JUST A CLOSER WALK

with thee

OVERCOMING CHRISTIAN FORGETFULNESS WITH GOSPEL RHYTHMS

by

KRYSTAL KOLB

©2024 by Krystal Kolb

Published by hope*books
2217 Matthews Township Pkwy
Suite D302
Matthews, NC 28105
www.hopebooks.com

hope*books is a division of hope*media
Printed in the United States of America

All rights reserved. Without limiting the rights under copyrights reserved above, no part of this publication may be scanned, uploaded, reproduced, distributed, or transmitted in any form or by any means whatsoever without express prior written permission from both the author and publisher of this book—except in the case of brief quotations embodied in critical articles and reviews.

First Edition

Thank you for supporting the author's rights.

First paperback edition.
Paperback ISBN: 979-8-89185-101-6
Hardcover ISBN: 979-8-89185-102-3
Ebook ISBN: 979-8-89185-103-0
Library of Congress Number: 2024942138

All Scripture quotations, unless otherwise indicated, are taken from the Holy Bible, New International Version®, NIV®. Copyright ©1973, 1978, 1984, 2011 by Biblica, Inc.™ Used by permission of Zondervan. All rights reserved worldwide. www.zondervan.com The "NIV" and "New International Version" are trademarks registered in the United States Patent and Trademark Office by Biblica, Inc.™

hb
hope*books
hopebooks.com
*Because the world needs your hope filled
words now more than ever*

To Emily, Caleb, Nora, and Elizabeth

May you grow in the grace and knowledge of our Lord and Savior Jesus Christ. To Him be glory both now and forever! Amen.

2 Peter 3:18

Contents

Introduction	1
We Forget: God Has A Purpose for Our Lives	9
Gospel Rhythm: Reading Scripture	21
We Forget: We Need Forgiveness	35
Gospel Rhythm: Repentance	49
We Forget: We Are Forgiven	61
Gospel Rhythm: Prayer	73
We Forget: In This World We Will Have Trouble	87
Gospel Rhythm: Living Life in the Christian Community	101
We Forget: True Joy is Only Found in God	115
Gospel Rhythm: Surrender	127
We Forget: God Is Always With Us	139
Gospel Rhythm: Praise	153
We Forget: Our Time is Limited	165
Gospel Rhythm: Repeat Gospel Truths	175
Epilogue	189
Acknowledgments	191
References	193

Introduction

"A great many think because they have been filled once, they are going to be full for all time after; but, O, my friends, we are leaky vessels, and have to be kept right under the fountain all the time in order to keep full...Let us come near Him." -D.L. Moody

My children and I were on our way to M.O.P.S. (Mothers of Preschool Students) when my daughter asked for the fourth time on our short drive, "Where are we going?" I wondered how she could forget where we were going so many times on such a short drive. God used this interaction to minister to my own heart. Her repeated questions made me realize that I often forget the rich truths that God has placed in my life.

The Christian walk has felt a bit wobbly to me. I don't have a specific time when I knew I became a Christian, but I have the assurance that I am a Christian because the Holy Spirit is working in my life. Even though I am certain that I am a child of God, my growth hasn't been linear. I have felt high highs and low lows. I end up getting off the path more than I ever want to and I need to return to my heavenly Father over and over again. I forget that I can't live life on my own. I need to be reminded that this world is not my home, and I get stuck in sin and shame more often than I would like to admit. I have learned that the Christian walk is not a straight one. Not everything is going to go perfectly for me and I need to cling to Jesus as I live out my days.

Here are some of the truths I often forget:

- I am forgiven and God sees me with Jesus's righteousness, not with my sin stains.
- God is always with me. There is nothing that I undertake without the Holy Spirit's presence with me.
- True joy is only found in God. I often forget and try to substitute God's gifts and things of this world for my joy supply.
- I will not do everything perfectly, nor will all of my circumstances go the way that I want them to.
- God has a purpose and a plan for my life. My life is to be used for His glory.

What about you? Do you forget the truths God has laid on your heart? Do you have a hard time remembering what your devotions were about? Do you feel like your emotions take control when you get pressed? Do you constantly second guess that God loves and cares for you?

As Christians, we have an enemy that does not want us to remember God's truths in our lives. The Bible says this about Satan:

INTRODUCTION

"Be alert and of sober mind. Your enemy the devil prowls around like a roaring lion looking for someone to devour. Resist him, standing firm in the faith, because you know that the family of believers throughout the world is undergoing the same kind of sufferings."
1 Peter 5:7-9

"The thief comes to steal, kill, and destroy; I have come that they may have life, and have it to the full."
John 10:10

Satan twists the truth and makes us second guess whether God has our good in mind. Satan also makes us second-guess God's glory. We start to wonder if God is as powerful, mighty, loving, and just as He claims to be. We see this already in the third chapter of the Bible when Satan starts whispering in Eve's ear:

"Now the serpent was more crafty than any of the wild animals the Lord God had made. He said to the woman, 'Did God really say, "You must not eat from any tree in the garden"?'"
Genesis 3:1

We see here the serpent's craftiness and how we tend to forget what God said and start to second-guess God's motives. The same crafty serpent that whispered in Eve's ear all those years ago is whispering in our ears today. He wants to pull us away from the rich truths that God offers us. He wants our hearts to be anxious and unwilling to trust God's promises.

It would be easy to give a list of actions that you can take to resolve this forgetfulness problem. Just do "this, this, and this," and then you will never forget God or His amazing promises. Our Christian walk doesn't work like that. We can't do anything to save ourselves. When I realize that I have forgotten these basic Christian truths, I tend to beat myself up. I often think that I should know better or that I should be further along by now. These thoughts come straight from the enemy. My hope in writing this book is that when we realize that we are forgetful and we have forgotten again, we use that as an opportunity to cry out to the God who saves us so that we don't sink into a pit of despair.

The Bible tells us to remember one hundred thirty times in the Old Testament and thirty-six times in the New Testament. God wants us to remember, and reminds us again and again that He remembers His promises. King David sums it up well:

> *"On my bed I remember you;*
> *I think of you through the watches of the night."*
> Psalm 63:6

David remembered God throughout his days. I think we can start thinking that remembering is up to us as well. We can't remember God on our own either. Jesus tells us:

> *"Remain in me, and I will remain in you. No branch can bear fruit by itself; it must remain in the vine. Neither can you bear fruit unless you remain in me."*
> John 15:4

How the Book Is Set-Up:

This book is set up in a pattern with two different styles of chapters: forgetfulness and gospel rhythms. The chapters will alternate between what we forget and move into a gospel rhythm to help us abide in God. Just as a day moves from darkness to light, this book will begin with the dark things we forget and move to

INTRODUCTION

God's hope and light in the darkness with a gospel rhythm. The forgetfulness chapters will help us to see that we can easily stray from God. The gospel rhythm chapters are designed to help us to lift up our eyes so that we can see God.

> "I lift my eyes up to you, to you who sit enthroned in heaven."
> Psalm 123:1

Enter Through the Wicket Gate

When we know that we are God's children, we are free to carry out God's purpose in our lives. In John Bunyan's book *Pilgrim's Progress*, there is a man named Christian who goes on a journey that represents the Christian walk. Christian meets a man named Evangelist who tells him he must enter through the Wicket Gate. After passing through the Wicket Gate, Christian experiences forgiveness for his sins and new life through faith in Jesus. Later he encounters others on the path who were trying to climb over the fence instead of going through the Wicket Gate. The others were not able to get to the end of the journey to the Celestial City the way that Christian did because they didn't enter through the Wicket Gate. Friends, we must enter through the Wicket Gate as well. Trusting in Jesus for the forgiveness of our sins is the only way that we are going to receive God's salvation and the only way He will work in our lives. We can't take shortcuts here. We must enter through the Wicket Gate.[1]

Before we begin discussing our Christian sin patterns, we need to first make sure that we are Christians. There are three ways that we can know if we are Christians:

1.) We understand the depth of our sin and know that we need a Savior.

> *"Jesus replied, 'Very truly I tell you, everyone who sins is a slave to sin. Now a slave has no permanent place in the family, but a son belongs to it forever. So if the Son sets you free, you will be free indeed.'"*
> John 8:34-36

The Holy Spirit allows us to understand that we need a Savior. We are all born with a sinful nature that separates us from God. I spent many years thinking that I was "good enough" and subtly thinking I didn't need a Savior in my life. We can't be saved until we see the weight of our sin and turn to Jesus in repentance for our only help. We will discuss this more in a future chapter.

2.) We repent and put our faith in Jesus to save us from our sins. We believe that the work of Jesus on the cross is what removed our sins from us.

> *"Since the children have flesh and blood, he too shared in their humanity so that by his death he might break the power of him who holds the power of death—that is, the devil— and free those who all their lives were held in slavery by their fear of death."*
> Hebrews 2:14-15

Jesus came to the world as a man and never sinned, suffered a horrible death as payment for our sins, and was raised back to life and now sits at the right hand of God the Father interceding for us. We are in bondage to our sin until we trust that Jesus's blood covers it. We put our hope in Jesus, not in ourselves.

3.) We have the deposit of the Holy Spirit working in our lives.

INTRODUCTION

"The Spirit you received does not make you slaves, so that you live in fear again; rather, the Spirit you received brought about your adoption to sonship. And by him we cry, 'Abba, Father.' The Spirit himself testifies with our spirit that we are God's children."
Romans 8:15-16

"Now it is God who makes both us and you stand firm in Christ. He anointed us, set his seal of ownership on us, and put his Spirit in our hearts as a deposit, guaranteeing what is to come."
2 Corinthians 1:21-22

Before Jesus ascended to Heaven, He told the disciples that it would be good for Him to go so that they could have the Holy Spirit (John 16:7). The Holy Spirit is active in the world today in the lives of those who believe in Jesus. We can have assurance that we are in Jesus when we feel the Holy Spirit's promptings in our lives. The Holy Spirit will convict us of sin, help us to understand Scripture, and provide discernment as we walk in our daily lives. If you are being led by the Holy Spirit, you can have assurance that you are in Jesus because we don't receive the Holy Spirit unless we are God's children (Romans 8:14-16).

How do we enter through the Wicket Gate? We go back to our three steps from earlier: 1.) We see that our sins are many and that they separate us from God. If you are having trouble seeing the burden of your sins, I would pray and ask God to convict your heart. 2.) We trust that Jesus dying on the cross was for us and repent of our sins. 3.) We receive the benefit of the Holy Spirit and walk in step with the Spirit.

Let's look at two important definitions as we close out this section:

Justification: The one-time payment of Jesus on the cross that takes away the sins of those who trust in Him and allows us to be saved.

Sanctification: The continual process of becoming more and more like Jesus. We sin, then we are convicted of our sin, and then we repent and keep walking with Jesus along the way.

This book will mostly be about the sanctification process in our lives, but I do want to make sure that you are assured of your justification in Jesus. We can't receive any of Jesus's benefits without His justification. Then, when we are justified, we can trust Him to sanctify us day by day.

I hope that you will join me as we discuss the things we forget as Christians. When we realize we have forgotten again, I want to remind us, with gospel rhythms, that we are right where we need to be; in the arms of our Savior.

We Forget: God Has A Purpose for Our Lives

"Our greatest fear should not be of failure, but of succeeding at things in life that don't really matter."
-D.L. Moody

Introduction

*I*magine with me for a second that a basketball coach is giving his team the game plan. Part of that game plan is to key in on one of the best players on the opposing team and try to make that player commit a foul, forcing them out of the game. The best player on the other team "fouling out" could be helpful in winning the game, but it isn't the true purpose of the game. The purpose of the game is to score more points than the other team. There are many ways that a basketball team could win the game. If the team does succeed in "fouling out" the best player on the other team, but they don't stop the other players from scoring and they don't score themselves, they are missing the whole point of the game.

I think we do this in our lives as well. We often miss the true purpose for living our Christian lives. We get so focused on building the lives that we want that we often miss the point of what God intends for us.

I am often guilty of forgetting that I was created on purpose and for a purpose. The testimony of how I came to faith in Christ is pretty unremarkable by the world's standards, but the fact that I am in Christ is unbelievably remarkable! I grew up in the church, my parents raised me to know Jesus, and I tried to be obedient to Him for the majority of my life. While I was growing up in the church and learning about Jesus, I was also following what modern culture would have for my life. I wanted to fit in with others around me and I wasn't rooted in God's Word. Any idea that came my way wasn't tested by God's Word, it was tested by what the culture said. I was a nominal Christian, a Christian in name only. I knew what Jesus did for me, but I didn't understand the weight of my sin and I was believing many of the lies the world was feeding me.

Fast-forward to adult life. After getting married and having children, our marriage goals were primarily cultural. Our goals for our kids were that they would be happy and grow up to fit in with everyone else. I wanted them to get good jobs, marry good people, and be "successful" in the world's eyes. We brought them to church and taught them the Sunday School Bible stories, but we weren't actually teaching them to know and love Jesus.

Somewhere around 2017, my husband, Peter, and I started reading the Bible together. We read the Scriptures in their entirety. During that year, both of our lives were transformed. It was like scales fell from our eyes and we could see clearly the weight of our sin for the first time. When we began to realize how heavy our sin was, we realized the depth of the gift that Jesus gave to us. In response, we wanted to serve Him with our lives. Suddenly the things we cared about before became less meaningful and we started to live for Jesus instead of ourselves. (This is a process, which we are still working on.)

We realized that our lives were not being lived with purpose. Our parenting changed from wanting worldly desires for our kids to wanting to truly train them in the Lord. We started spending our money differently. We started supporting children through Compassion International and desired for God's Word to reach the ends of the earth. We made sure to tithe at church, which we weren't committed to before. Our choices in entertainment changed and we started being more careful about what we watched with each other and as a family. We also desired that others would turn to Jesus in their own lives and we wanted to have more gospel-saturated conversations rather than small talk. Our behaviors and desires changed because God did a work in our hearts.

I am describing my old life to you because it was the perfect illustration of purposelessness. God has given me a purpose, and for the majority of my life, I was not fulfilling that purpose. I think many people are stuck in this same purposeless cycle. We go to work, educate our children, and run through the motions of life each day without actually thinking about why we are here. We forget that God has a purpose for our lives.

God Made Us To Glorify Him

Answering the question, "Why am I here?" is actually more simple than we make it out to be. Christians throughout the ages asked these questions too, and in response, they created Catechisms. Catechisms are a series of questions and answers that teach us the doctrines of our faith in Jesus that help to summarize what we learn in Scripture. There are many different versions and I have found them to be very helpful in understanding the basics of the Christian faith.

Let's start with the New City Catechism. Question 4 asks this: "How and why did God create us?" The answer: "God created us male and female in His own image to glorify Him."[2] That's it. A very simple answer to a very profound question. What is my purpose here on earth? My purpose is to glorify God. The way that we glorify God is going to look different for everyone, but the purpose is the same. We were created to glorify God!

The Westminster Catechism question 1 asks this: "What is the chief end of man?" The answer: "Man's chief end is to glorify God, and to enjoy Him forever."[3] This is very similar to the New City Catechism except that it says we should enjoy Him forever!

What does it look like to glorify God and enjoy Him forever? We have reminders every day of God's love and faithfulness. The sun rises every morning and sets every night, there is beauty in creation all around us, the seasons change, the people we love bring us delight and remind us of God's goodness, and God has given us His Word that reveals Himself to us. We glorify God when we take notice of the things that God reveals to us. We should take notice that the sun rose this morning and glorify God for it! We should look into our loved one's eyes and give glory to God for them. We should read the Bible and meditate on the words God has written to us. We also glorify God by obeying His commands because we know that they are what is best for us.

Glorifying God in my own life looks like keeping a thankfulness journal and expressing gratitude for how He has blessed my life. Filling my home with hymns and worship music as I do the daily activities of life helps me to remember all the wonders of God's character and I can send that praise right back to Him. I try to walk as Jesus did in my relationships and I want to be His representative in the lives of my loved ones. This also means apologizing to my loved ones when I fail to walk as Jesus did, which is often. As I walk through my days, I try to ask myself this question: "How can I glorify God right now?" Usually, an answer finds me and I can walk in obedience to what God has for my day.

> *"So whether you eat or drink or whatever you do, do it all for the glory of God."*
> 1 Corinthians 10:31

Obey God's Commands

The Heidelberg Catechism Question 4 asks this: "What does God's law require of us?" The answer: "Christ teaches us this in summary in Matthew 22–

Love the Lord your God with all your heart and with all your soul and with all your mind and with all your strength. This is the first and greatest commandment and the second is like it: Love your neighbor as yourself. All the Law and the Prophets hang on these two commandments."[4]

Part of fulfilling our purpose of glorifying God is obeying God's laws, which we learn about in His Word. We know that because of our sin nature, we will not be able to obey them perfectly, but we strive to obey them in this life with the Holy Spirit's help because we love God and want to glorify Him! Out of gratitude for Him, we obey. It is not only for our good that we obey God's commands but also for the good of those around us.

Make Disciples of All the Nations
Another part of glorifying God is making disciples. As Jesus was ascending into Heaven He told His disciples this: "All authority in heaven and on earth has been given to me. Therefore go and make disciples of all nations, baptizing them in the name of the Father and of the Son and of the Holy Spirit, and teaching them to obey everything I have commanded you. And surely I am with you always, to the very end of the age" (Matthew 28:18-20).

These last words of Jesus on earth are a challenge and a comfort. Jesus has all authority and shares it with those who are trusting in Him for their salvation. He tells us our duty is to go and make disciples of all the nations and all the authority in Heaven and on earth that Jesus has will be shared with us to help us carry out that command. This means that if we are a disciple of Jesus, our mission is to be disciple-makers. Our hearts should be for those who are lost and don't know the love of Jesus in their lives. Jesus promised to help us as we spend our lives on a mission to make disciples of all the nations.

What Does Living With a Purpose Look Like?

Before we begin seeing how this looks in real life, I want to remind us that we need to enter through the Wicket Gate, just like Christian in *Pilgrim's Progress*. Our lives will not be lived with purpose if we do not trust in Jesus for the forgiveness of our sins and the Holy Spirit's help to guide us on our path. "Unless the Lord builds the house, the builders labor in vain. Unless the Lord watches over the city, the guards stand watch in vain. In vain you rise early and stay up late, toiling for food to eat—for he grants sleep to those he loves" (Psalm 127:1-2). Unless we are living purposefully for God and in His strength, the things we are doing won't really matter.

The beginning of this poem by C.T. Studd sums up this sentiment:

"Only one life, 'twill soon be past,

Only what's done for Christ will last."[5]

The Bible makes it clear that God has work for us to do while we are here on earth. "For we are God's handiwork, created in Christ Jesus to do good works, which God prepared in advance for us to do" (Ephesians 2:10). One of the best things about being a Christian is getting to serve God. When we complete the good works that God has for us, it fills us up and gives us purpose and joy. God doesn't give us a license to do whatever we want as soon as we become His child. No, He gives us joy by allowing us to complete His work here on earth.

"Each of you should use whatever gift you have received to serve others, as faithful stewards of God's grace in its various forms" (1 Peter 4:10). God has work for us to do, but that work is going to look different for each of us. Some have the gift of teaching, hospitality, or service and those gifts from God should be used to bless the church and glorify God. Even though we may be gifted in certain areas, we will also be called upon to serve in ways that we are not gifted. In those times, we are still called to give to the best of our ability.

Our purpose each day is to wake with open hands asking God to show us His will for that day. "Do not conform to the pattern of this world, but be transformed by the renewing of your mind. Then you will be able to test and approve what God's will is—His good, pleasing, and perfect will" (Romans 12:2). God has given each of us different giftings and life situations and we are called to glorify God on each of our unique journeys. God's will may not be perfectly clear to us at all times so we need to be transformed by the renewing of our mind. We need to be in prayer with God throughout our days asking for eyes to see what His good, pleasing, and perfect will is for us that day.

Maybe God's will is for you to have that uncomfortable conversation, or to leave your plan so that you can help someone in distress, or turn from your sin and pursue holiness, or to just spend some time thinking about God and His attributes. Each day we are met with an extensive amount of choices and it is hard to discern what we are supposed to be doing at any given time. We can trust that if we ask God to show us what He wants us to do, we know that He will also equip us to carry that task out. "And we know that in all things God works for the good of those who love him, who have been called according to his purpose" (Romans 8:28). Even though we don't always know the way God wants us to go, we can trust that He will be faithful to help us carry out His will, as well as illuminate the path as we walk.

The Heidelberg Catechism Question 32 asks this: "But why are you called a Christian?" Answer: "Because by faith I am a member of Christ and so I share in His anointing. I am anointed to confess His name, to present myself to Him as a living sacrifice of thanks, to strive with a good conscience against sin and the devil in this life, and afterward to reign with Christ over all creation for all eternity."[6]

Christians must live lives with purpose. This means we will be a picture of Christ to nonbelievers. They will see Jesus by how we live our lives. The Holy Spirit living in us allows us to reflect on the character of Jesus, tell others about Him, walk in His holiness, and work out our sanctification process while we walk this earth. We glorify God by reflecting His nature and walking in obedience to Him.

Example of Discerning Our Purpose

Let's imagine for a minute that you have a big decision to make in your life. You want to know if God wants you to marry that person, or if you should move to that city, or how many children you should have. We often want the path before us to be illuminated. We feel uncomfortable when we have unanswered questions.

Here are some steps you can take when you are unsure what choice God wants you to make:
1. We need to make sure that we are in alignment with Scripture. If the person we are set to marry isn't a

Christian, that doesn't align with Scripture and we shouldn't marry them. If moving to a different city or having more children is going to make you disobey Scripture, then you do not do that thing. God's Word is our guide that helps us determine which choices we should make.
2. When Scripture does not provide a clear answer, pray about it and ask God for discernment.
3. We listen to trusted friends and family that God has placed in our lives.

There are commands that we know God wants us to follow. We know that we should obey Scripture and worship God. If we are doing those things, we know that we are in alignment with God's will for our lives. "Now all has been heard; here is the conclusion of the matter: Fear God and keep his commandments, for this is the duty of all mankind" (Ecclesiastes 12:13). When we obey Scripture and worship God, our joy will flow freely and God will be glorified.

He is Worthy

You may be thinking, "Well, that seems kind of arrogant that God wants us to glorify Him with our days." If God were a mere man, it would be arrogant! But God isn't a mere man. God is God and He is worthy of all our worship. "For from him and through him and for him are all things. To him be the glory forever! Amen" (Romans 11:36). "You are worthy, our Lord and God, to receive glory and honor and power, for you created all things, and by your will they were created and have their being" (Revelation 4:11).

God not only deserves our praise, but He knows that it is to our benefit to give Him glory and praise. Our joy is made complete when we do what we were made to do: glorify God!

"You make known to me the path of life; you will fill me with joy in your presence, with eternal pleasures at your right hand."
Psalm 16:11

God sent Jesus to pay for our sins with His blood so that we could be reconciled to God and live as His children. After we are reconciled to God, we live lives with purpose. Let's not be like the basketball team that forgot its purpose. Our purpose is to glorify God in all that we do, obey His commands, and make disciples as we go. God doesn't want us to sit on our hands and do nothing. He gives us a purpose and that purpose leads to our joy! Praise God that we can live lives that matter and when we see Him in glory we can hear the words, "Well done, good and faithful servant" (Matthew 25:21).

HOW WE REMEMBER

Do you find yourself trying to fulfill the world's purpose for your life? Do you forget that your life is to be used to glorify God? Are you having trouble discerning what God wants you to do next?

- As you wake up to start each day, pray with open hands asking God what He wants for your day. Often we get so focused on our plan for the day that we forget that God has a purpose for us. When we spend time with God in prayer, we are reminded that God has a purpose for our day and we should walk in His purpose rather than our own.

Gospel Rhythm: Reading Scripture

> Contemporary people tend to examine the Bible, looking for things they can't accept; but Christians should reverse that, allowing the Bible to examine us, looking for things God can't accept.
> -Tim Keller

Introduction:

When you see that our first gospel rhythm is reading your Bible, you may be tempted to roll your eyes and say, "Yeah, yeah, I know that one already." This gospel rhythm may feel like a trite Sunday school answer to you. There is even a Sunday school song that says, "Read your Bible and pray every day, and you will grow, grow, grow." Reading your Bible is a common Sunday school answer because it is a primary method by which we can connect to God. The author of Hebrews tells it this way:

> *In the past God spoke to our forefathers through the prophets at many times and in various ways, but in these last days he has spoken to us by his Son, whom he appointed heir of all things, and through whom he made the universe.*
> Hebrews 1:1-2

Jesus spoke to us through His life as a living example, but Jesus is also called the Word in John 1:1: *"In the beginning was the Word, and the Word was with God, and the Word was God. He was with God in the beginning."* God's primary way of speaking to us now is not through prophets but through the Word of God. If we want to hear from God, we turn to His Word. His Word is what tethers us to Him amid a world of distractions and temptations.

The Bible is the most unique book you will find. It was written by 35 traditional authors over a period of 1,500 years, but it still tells one cohesive story. Not only does it have many different authors writing at different times, but the Bible is living and active. This book has divine power and the ability to change people to be more like Jesus. Reading God's Word is transforming and shapes our lives. Reading God's Word has been the primary means that God used to soften my own heart.

In my own life, reading the Bible has, hands down, transformed me more than any other thing I do. It has helped me to form a deeper relationship with God, it has helped me to understand my purpose, it has shown me my deep need for God, and it continues to convict me of my sin. It has also helped me to relate with other people in a manner pleasing to God. After the Apostle Paul was converted to Christianity, the Bible tells us that it was like scales fell from his eyes (Acts 9:18). I truly felt like scales fell from my eyes after being transformed by reading scripture. I could see the world in a completely different way, and it was amazing! I want that for others as well.

As I read through the Bible, sometimes I am brought to tears because God did something powerful in someone else's life. Sometimes, I will read something and know that I am in sin, and I will feel the need to repent. Sometimes, I just sit in the fact that God loves and cares for me and He is active in my life. I feel a proximity to God as if He is sitting in the same room talking to me rather than me reading it off the page.

It wasn't always that way for me. I spent the majority of my life with the Bible on my shelf. I wasn't opposed to hearing from Scripture in sermons and hymns, but I wasn't actively trying to understand what God was telling me through His Word. I somehow thought I could live a Christian life without Christ and His Word being my guide. God started nudging me to read the Bible through books I was reading and podcasts I was listening to. I kept hearing these nudges and talked to Peter about it, and we both started a Bible reading plan together. I don't have a moment where I know I became a Christian; I know that I am one, and I am not sure that I was back in the time when the Bible was on my shelf. If I was, I was rendered a useless one.

What is the One Story the Bible is Telling?
Reading the entire Bible can be intimidating. It is a huge book, and it can be hard to understand. But the Bible tells one big story. The story of Scripture begins with a loving Creator who brings forth a beautiful world with land, sea, animals, and humans from the words of His mouth. This world was perfect un-

til the humans He created rebelled against their loving Creator. For the first time, the humans felt guilt and shame and tried to hide from their Creator. From that time on, humanity continued to multiply, and more and more people filled the earth, but they were all under the curse of sin.

The rest of scripture tells about how the people on the earth continued to rebel and how God continued to pursue them. He promised to send His Son to save them from the horrible curse. The Old Testament gives predictions about the coming of Jesus, and then the New Testament tells the story of Jesus's coming and gives instructions about how our lives will look when we receive the gift of forgiveness of sins through Jesus' death on the cross.

Why Should I Read My Bible?

There are numerous reasons for reading your Bible, but I would like to address five reasons here.

1. Reading God's Word helps us to see His character and helps us draw near to Him. *"Open my eyes that I may see the wonderful truths in your law"* (Psalm 119:18). God's Word tells the story of a loving God who comes to save His people. His character is written on every page, and we can grow in the knowledge of who He is. The more we know God with our mind, the more we can love Him with our heart.
2. Reading God's Word helps in our battle against sin. *"For the Word of God is living and active. Sharper than any double-edged sword, it penetrates even to dividing soul and spirit, joints and marrow; it judges the thoughts and*

attitudes of the heart" (Hebrews 4:12). As we read the Bible, we are convicted of sin which leads us to repentance. *"How can a young person stay on the path of purity? By living according to Your word. I seek You with all my heart; do not let me stray from Your commands. I have hidden Your word in my heart that I might not sin against You. Praise be to You, Lord; teach me Your decrees. With my lips I recount all the laws that come from Your mouth. I rejoice in following Your statutes as one rejoices in great riches. I meditate on Your precepts and consider Your ways. I delight in Your decrees; I will not neglect Your word" (Psalm 119:9-16).* God gives us limits and boundaries because He loves us and knows what is best for us. The more we read God's Word, the more we see the best way for us to go.

3. Reading God's Word helps us to have hope. The future looks pretty bleak without God's promises of eternal life with Him. *"For everything that was written in the past was written to teach us, so that through endurance and the encouragement of the Scriptures we might have hope" (Romans 15:4).* We can look to God's Word to encourage us and strengthen us in the hope of Jesus.

4. Reading God's Word protects us from false teaching. *"For there will come a time when men will not put up with sound doctrine. Instead, to suit their own desires, they will gather around them a great number of teachers to say what their itching ears want to hear. They will turn their ears away from the truth and turn aside to myths" (2 Timothy 4:3-4).* The world is filled with many different ideas about how we should live our lives and what "the good

life" is. God's Word tells us the truth about who we are and illuminates the path for our feet so we know where to walk. *"Your word is a lamp to my feet and a light for my path" (Psalm 119:105).* God's Word will not lead us astray like the false teachings of the world can.

5. Finally, God's Word helps us to know the truth. *"Heaven and earth will pass away, but My words will never pass away" (Mark 13:31).* God's Word is the lasting truth that we can rely on as we walk through this world. *"But as for you, continue in what you have learned and have become convinced of, because you know those from whom you learned it, and how from infancy you have known the holy Scriptures, which are able to make you wise for salvation through faith in Christ Jesus" (2 Timothy 3:14-15).*

What if I Don't Desire to Read My Bible or Understand the Bible?

One of the major complaints about scripture reading is that our desire to read it may wane. We won't always come to read God's Word with excited and expectant hearts. This can get us stuck because we think that our emotions should be right there with us all the time. That isn't always the case. Sometimes, we need to just complete the task because we know it is the right thing to do. As you make a habit of reading God's Word, your emotions will follow.

This has been true in my life. There have been plenty of times when I haven't understood the Bible and didn't want to read it because it was very confusing. Hello Daniel and Revelation! The more I come back to scripture, the more I want to come back to scripture. We will crave what we feed ourselves. If we feed ourselves what the culture says, we will believe everything the culture says. If we feed ourselves God's Word, we will crave and want to know God's Word.

Jen Wilkin gives good wisdom about Bible reading:

> *"Some days your study may not move you emotionally or speak to an immediate need. You may not be able to apply the passage to all. But what if ten years from now, in a dark night of the soul, that passage suddenly opens up to you because of the work you have done today? Wouldn't your long-term investment be worth it?"[7]*

I remember a time when I longed for the Bible to transform my life; It was at the funeral of one of my loved ones who had been buried with her Bible. I wondered if I would ever love God's Word as much as she did. Years later, I do. I love God's Word. It is a compass and a light for my path. I can't live in this world without it. If you are feeling like you would like to love God's Word but don't feel like you do, my suggestion would be to ask. Ask God to deepen your affection for His Word.

How to Read Your Bible

The Bible can be a very confusing book. It is also a very large book, which can be intimidating to pick up and try to read in its entirety. When we understand that the Bible is a main source of nourishment that God gives us and is better for us to read than any other book (including this one), we should make it a point to read it and know what it says. I suggest reading your Bible in two different ways.

Breadth/Depth
1. For Breadth - this means that you should read the entire Bible to get an understanding of what is in this book. Once you have read through the entire Bible, you can see that there are different types of books inside the Bible. There are books on history, law, poetry, wisdom, prophecy, gospels, letters, and even apocalyptic literature. All of these types of literature point to one big story about God sending His Son to save us from our sins. When you read all of Scripture, you can see how these pieces work together to tell that one story. I also find when I read the Bible in its entirety, I am at different points in my life when I revisit passages. Sometimes, the passages will hit me differently because of the different circumstances going on around me. We want to revisit the whole of Scripture over and over again.

Some ways we can read for breadth or understanding of the Bible as a whole:

- Find a yearly Bible reading plan. It is nice to approach Scripture with a plan rather than trying to figure out each day what you should read. When you come with a plan, you can get started right away and focus on what you are reading instead of where in the Bible you should read.
- The Bible Project has video summaries for each book of the Bible. Before digging into each book, you can watch a short video to receive an overview of the book and helpful areas to look for as you read.[8]

2. For Depth - We want to know the whole of Scripture, but we also want to dig in and truly understand the message the original authors intended to convey. We want to read it over and over again so God's Word sinks deep into our hearts, and we have it readily available as we encounter needs along the way. When we read for depth we are taking a book of the Bible and studying it and sometimes memorizing it so we can take it with us on life's journey. In my own life, there has been no greater cutting to my heart than reading Scripture for depth. When I slow down and really look at what a passage is telling me, it gets to my heart. I am forced to search my heart and see if my life matches with what I am reading.

Some ways you can read for depth:

- I have found Jen Wilkin's Bible studies on different books of the Bible to be very helpful, as well as her book *Women of the Word*.

Three Questions as You Read

As we read through Scripture, we should always ask ourselves these questions:

1. What is this passage telling me about God? - The Bible is a book about God, so each passage should have plenty to inform us of Him. One thing I have done as I read Scripture as a whole is to highlight the passages that tell about God and His character in green. You can use whatever color you want, but I love opening my Bible and seeing the green highlights that tell me that I am

going to see God's character in whatever passage I am reading.
2. What does this passage tell me about myself in relation to God? The Bible is helpful in showing us our place with God. We often tend to think that we are more important than what we actually are. We want to rule our own lives, and we want to be praised. God's Word shows us that God is in control of our lives, and He is the one worthy of praise.
3. How can I apply this passage to my life? The Bible gives us numerous applications to our own lives. We should look in every passage for understanding and wisdom on how to live in light of what that passage was telling us.

The S.O.A.P. Method

This method of reading Scripture was developed by Pastor Wayne Cordeiro and helps us pull more out of the text as we read. Before you begin reading, you can pray to God to open your eyes that you may see the wonderful truths in His law (Psalm 119:18).

Scripture (S)- As you read through the passage, pull out specific verses that stand out to you. These verses will be able to help you remember the passage as well as be good verses to memorize and meditate on. When we read a full chapter or any length of a passage that is longer than a few verses, it is hard for us to remember everything that is said. When we pull out a verse or two that captures the essence of the passage, we can take that with us throughout the day.

***Observe (O)*-** As you read you should know the context from the Bible. You should know who wrote the book and who they are communicating with. You should know what kind of literature you are reading. This section helps us to familiarize ourselves with the text. We want to know in general what is being communicated and why.

***Apply (A)*-** This is where we take what we are reading and put it into action. We are able to put our faith into action based on what God's Word is telling us to do. The Bible has numerous applications. This section is helpful for us to gain wisdom and understanding.

***Pray (P)*-** When we are finished we take what we read back to God and pray over what He is communicating to us in our reading that day. We could pray back verses that we picked out from the Scripture section or we can just spend time telling God about what we learned that day.

Formed by God's Word, Not by the Culture

We want God's Word to shape and form us, not the culture around us. When we are rooted in God's Word, we won't be blown about by any new idea that comes floating our way. This line from the hymn "On Christ the Solid Rock I Stand" is a good reminder for my soul: "In every high and stormy gale, my anchor holds within the veil." The winds will come, and when they do, we want to be tethered to the anchor, Jesus Christ. We do that by soaking in His Word.

We can learn lessons in the present from God's Word. God can teach us through what He taught His people in the past. When the Israelites (God's chosen people) were leaving slavery in Egypt and were about ready to go into God's promised land with Joshua leading them, God gave these instructions:

> "Be strong and very courageous. Be careful to obey all the law my servant Moses gave you; do not turn from it to the right or to the left, that you may be successful wherever you go. Keep this Book of the Law always on your lips; meditate on it day and night, so that you may be careful to do everything written in it. Then you will be prosperous and successful. Have I not commanded you? Be strong and courageous. Do not be afraid; do not be discouraged, for the Lord your God will be with you wherever you go."
> Joshua 1:7-9

God told them to be strong and courageous, and right after, He told them to keep the Book of the Law always on their lips, meditating on it day and night. We have God's instructions with us wherever we go; we should make sure that we receive the great benefit of God's Word as well. We should meditate on it day and night so we know where to go and what to do in this world. When I read scripture, I will pick out a verse or two that really stands out to me. I will write them in my prayer journal, and then I will read them over and over again throughout the month. Meditating on scripture means we are thinking about it and asking God how He would like our lives to be shaped by these verses.

Reading scripture is one of the best gospel rhythms to practice because it is the primary way that God speaks to His people. Scripture is a guide, a light, and a comfort for our path. Reading scripture is one of the best ways to prevent Christian forgetfulness in our lives.

HOW WE REMEMBER

How about you? Does Bible reading intimidate you? Do you worry that you don't feel anything when you come to meet with God through Scripture? Is it hard to understand the Scriptures?

Here are two things you can do.

1. Find a good Bible reading plan.
   a. The best way to keep moving on reading Scripture is to have a plan. Often, we can come to God's Word with no plan, and we end up wasting time looking for what we should read that day. If you have a Bible reading plan, it takes the guesswork out of it for you, and you can spend your time soaking up the Scripture rather than questioning where you should read.
2. Memorize and Meditate on Scripture.
   a. I love that God's Word is so portable. Memorizing Scripture is a great way to take God's Word with you in every situation you are in. As you read through God's Word, pull out verses that you can meditate on and memorize to help you remember God throughout your days.
3. Listen to good teaching on the Scriptures.
   a. Good teaching is saturated in Scripture and taught with passion and truth. This means that the message from one passage must align with the rest of scripture. A prayerful Christian community can be helpful in pointing to powerful and effective biblical teachers.

We Forget: We Need Forgiveness

> *"Until Sin Be Bitter, Christ Will Not Be Sweet."*
> -Thomas Watson

Introduction

This past year I was diagnosed with celiac disease, which means that my body produces an autoimmune response to gluten. The only treatment is to cut gluten out of my diet. If celiac disease is left untreated, it can cause damage to my organs and can cause cancer to grow. I was living my life happily eating gluten without understanding the damage that it was doing to my body. Just as I didn't understand the damage gluten was causing, sin in my life caused major damage as well. I was happily living my life, thinking that I was "good enough" and not fully understanding that my sin separated me from a holy God and blinded me from seeing my need for a Savior.

The sin in our lives is very deceptive. Satan often tries to trick us into thinking that we would have it better if we acted out against God's good plan for our lives. Satan wants us to think that God just wants to hold us back from our desires. Satan also wants to blind us to the harmfulness of our sin so that we don't see our own sin for what it is - a pathway to death. Just as I had no idea that eating gluten was hurting my body, we also are blind to how offensive our sin is to God.

I grew up going to church and I don't remember a time when I didn't know about God. I lived a moral life and when I sinned, I deemed my sins as "minor" compared to those around me. My identity was in being "the good girl" during my school years. Teachers seemed to enjoy having me in class and I liked being the one that the teachers could count on. Years later, when Peter and I started the process of reading God's Word, my heart was convicted of pride and I could see how far short I fell of God's standard for my life. Reading the Bible revealed to me my guilt and my need for a Savior. Just like a doctor had to diagnose me with celiac disease, God's Word revealed my sin sickness and my need for a Savior.

There is an old anecdote that claims if a bear is chasing you in the woods, you don't need to be the fastest person, you just can't be the slowest. I have wrongly adopted this same concept in my Christian walk. I often compare myself to others around me and think, "At least I'm not like her" or "I could never do what he did." I treat my faith like God is grading on a curve; if I have a higher grade than others, then I should be fine. I subconsciously think that if I have the moral high ground on others, then I should escape judgment. I also start to think that I deserve to be saved by God on my own merit. God's Word tells a different story.

WE FORGET: WE NEED FORGIVENESS

> *"For whoever keeps the whole law and yet stumbles at one point is guilty of breaking all of it."*
> *James 2:10*

God, in His mercy, helped me to see that my sin is offensive to Him. Only when God opened my eyes to my need for repentance and forgiveness in Him did I start to understand that I don't have the moral high ground on anyone. We all need to be saved by Jesus, not our good works. I think the rich lyrics to the old hymn *Amazing Grace* describe God's mercy in showing sinners their need for Him: *"I once was lost, but now am found; was blind, but now I see."* We are unable to see the offense of our sin until God shows us. When God does show us our sin, our response should be quick repentance.

Thomas Watson sums it up well: "Until sin be bitter, Christ will not be sweet." Our sin is bitter and when we see how bitter it is, we should feel the depth of the sweetness of Jesus. I went many years thinking that the cross was nice but not really understanding that Jesus suffered and died for me. When I see that *"It was my sin that held him there,"* from the beautiful hymn "How Deep the Father's Love for Us,"[9] I feel gratitude for the love of Jesus that has been lavished upon me. If I don't believe that Jesus had to die on the cross for my sins, I miss His love for me as well.

Offense of Sin

God's Word is like a mirror that shows us our true condition. The world will fill us with lies about who we are. God's Word tells us the truth about who God is and who we are. The idea that we don't need Jesus as our Savior is from the world. The Bible tells us that the only way to salvation is through Jesus. Jesus said, "I am the way, and the truth, and the life. No one comes to the Father except through me" (John 14:6). We can't receive life in God the Father unless we receive forgiveness in Jesus. We often fool ourselves into thinking that we deserve God as our Father by living a mostly moral life and volunteering our time for worthy efforts, but our sin separates us and we can't be reconciled until we receive the sacrifice of Jesus on the cross.

We often try to convince ourselves that on our own we are mostly good. God's Word reveals that on our own we are corrupt. We have sin-sick hearts that need to be repaired. Romans 3:10-12 says, "There is no one righteous, not even one; there is no one who understands, no one who seeks God. All have turned away, they have become worthless; there is no one who does good, not even one." And Romans 3:23 says, "For all have sinned and fall short of the glory of God."

We run into trouble when we don't see our sin as offensive to a perfectly holy God, but justify our sins by comparing them to the sins of others. The problem with this type of thinking is that it blinds us to our need for God's forgiveness, measuring our status before God in the same manner that the world judges. Rather, we should measure ourselves against God's Word. If we look to the world, more than likely we can find someone we are "ahead of," but God's Word reveals our true position. Our position in life is not in relation to other people but in relation to where we are with God. If we sin even once, we are separated from God.

Thomas Aquinas said: "*The magnitude of the punishment (of sin) matches the magnitude of the sin. Now a sin that is against God is infinite; the higher the person against whom it is committed, the graver the sin—it is more criminal to strike a head of state than a private citizen—and God is of infinite greatness. Therefore an infinite punishment is deserved for a sin committed against Him."*[8]

To put Thomas Aquinas's statement into the context of today, we see that it would be a greater offense to strike a police officer than one of our siblings. A student striking the principal of the school would be a greater offense than striking another student. When we sin, we sin against a holy, perfect God. The magnitude of God's supreme holiness makes even "minor" (to us) sins, "major" sins. Adam and Eve eating fruit in a garden doesn't seem like a "major" sin, but it was a sin against God, and therefore, a "major" sin and deserving of infinite punishment.

When our eyes are opened to the offense of our own sin, we realize that we have great need. This needy position primes us to look to God for help. Not many people want to be needy, but according to God, needy is exactly what we need to be to cry out to Him for help. We must recognize that we can't save ourselves.

Sweetness of Christ

The main benefit of crying out to God for help is receiving forgiveness for our sins. What does it look like when we are forgiven of our sins? Ephesians 2:1-10 gives us a helpful example of the gospel of Jesus:

> *"As for you, you were dead in your transgressions and sins, in which you used to live when you followed the ways of this world and of the ruler of the kingdom of the air, the spirit who is now at work in those who are disobedient. All of us also lived among them at one time, gratifying the cravings*

of our flesh and following its desires and thoughts. Like the rest, we were by nature deserving of wrath. But because of his great love for us, God, who is rich in mercy, made us alive with Christ even when we were dead in transgressions—it is by grace you have been saved. And God raised us up with Christ and seated us with him in the heavenly realms in Christ Jesus, in order that in the coming ages he might show the incomparable riches of his grace, expressed in his kindness to us in Christ Jesus. For it is by grace you have been saved, through faith—and this is not from yourselves, it is the gift of God—not by works, so that no one can boast. For we are God's handiwork, created in Christ Jesus to do good works, which God prepared in advance for us to do."

We are born into sin and we can't save ourselves from the depths of sin's grasp. We can't even recognize how sinful we are. Only a perfect Savior can provide rescue for us. Once we realize that we are dead and can't help ourselves, we see the sweetness of Jesus. God wants to show us the incomparable riches of His grace, expressed in His kindness to us in Christ Jesus (Ephesians 2:7). Just take a breath for a second and let that soak in. God wants to give us riches and He gives them by way of the kindness of Jesus to us on the cross. When we put our faith in Jesus, we are made new – our sins are removed from us. We are then able to do good works because Jesus lives in us and allows us to accomplish His purposes in our lives.

One of the most amazing aspects of the cross is that our offensive sin is removed from us as far as the east is from the west (Psalm 103:12). God put our sins on Jesus, and Jesus paid the price for all of our sins. They are gone! Now when God sees us, He sees us with Jesus's righteousness.

> "God made him who had no sin to be sin for us, so that in Him we might become the righteousness of God."
> 2 Corinthians 5:21

How sweet it is to be raised to new life in Christ after being dead in sin. How sweet it is to live the rest of our days with a Savior helping us to do the good works He has prepared for us to do. This is the gospel and this is our reason to celebrate! When I was convicted of my sin by reading the whole of Scripture, I felt free. God, in His love, convicted me of my sin and allowed me to repent and be washed clean of the sin I was carrying around with me. I don't have to be "good enough." I am a forgiven child of God, and I can walk in His ways because He will give me what I need to fulfill His commission.

Biblical Examples of Forgetting We Need Forgiveness

God's Word gives us examples of others who have gone before us and have stumbled with thinking they are more righteous and deserving than others. The Bible gives examples of people we want to imitate and examples of people we don't want to imitate. The Pharisees and Jonah are examples of people we don't want to imitate and David is an example of someone we do want to imitate.

The Pharisees

The Pharisees are the first example I would like to examine. These men were held in high regard and were zealous for God's Law. Their biggest issue was holding themselves with too high of esteem and not caring for others. We see an example of this in Luke 18:9-14:

> *"To some who were confident of their own righteousness and looked down on everybody else, Jesus told this parable: 'Two men went up to the temple to pray, one a Pharisee and the other a tax collector. The Pharisee stood up and prayed about himself: "God, I thank you that I am not like other men-robbers, evildoers, adulterers—or even like this tax collector. I fast twice a week and give a tenth of all I get." But the tax collector stood at a distance. He would not even look up to heaven, but beat his breast and said, "God, have mercy on me, a sinner." I tell you that this man, rather than the other, went home justified before God. For everyone who exalts himself will be humbled, and he who humbles himself will be exalted.'"*

The Pharisees were so busy trying to keep rules on the outside and appear good that they missed the whole point of living their lives to the glory of God. They missed their need for God. The Pharisees thought that they could keep all of God's commands and therefore not sin. The Pharisees were very prideful and thought they didn't need God. Pride is dangerous territory for the Pharisees and for us as well.

> *"In his pride the wicked does not seek him; in all his thoughts there is no room for God."*
> Psalm 10:4

> *"Pride goes before destruction, a haughty spirit before a fall."*
> Proverbs 16:18

> "Not that we are competent in ourselves to claim anything for ourselves, but our competence comes from God."
> 2 Corinthians 3:5

Jonah

The next example is Jonah. Jonah was instructed by God to go to Nineveh (a city of people who were enemies of Israel) and preach against them because God was going to bring destruction. Jonah didn't like that assignment because he was afraid that his enemies might repent and God would forgive them. Jonah ran in the opposite way of Nineveh to Tarshish instead. On his way to Tarshish, there was a storm and he told everyone to throw him overboard because he knew he was living in sin. He was swallowed by a big fish, stayed in the fish's belly for three days, and was spit out on the banks of Nineveh. He did what God asked after running away and was mad that the Ninevites repented. Jonah was a man who ran far from God in disobedience and still wanted to look down on the people of Nineveh as if they deserved God's judgment more than he did. The difference between the people of Nineveh and Jonah was quick repentance. When the people heard that judgment was coming, they repented immediately. Jonah had chance after chance to soften his heart and was still holding onto his pride when the book of Jonah ended.

We get an inside look at the state of Jonah's heart with this verse: "'I knew that you are a gracious and compassionate God, slow to anger and abounding in love, a God who relents from sending calamity. Now, Lord, take away my life, for it is better for me to die than to live.' But the Lord replied, 'Is it right for you to be angry?'" (Jonah 4:2-4). As you read through these verses you may be thinking: "These are good attributes of God, so why was Jonah so angry?" The answer is pride. He wanted good for himself because he thought that he deserved it. He desired destruction for the Ninevites because he believed that was what they deserved.

The truth is that nobody deserves God to be slow to anger and abounding in love. We don't deserve God to relent from sending us calamity because we have all fallen short of the glory of God (Romans 3:23). "We all, like sheep, have gone astray, each of us has turned to his own way; and the Lord has laid on Him the iniquity of us all" (Isaiah 53:6). Every single person walking the earth needs to be saved from their sins. We all need Jesus as our Savior.

David

King David fell deep into sin when he took a married woman out of his own desire. He then murdered her husband when he found out she was pregnant and knew his sins would be discovered. The following passage describes the prophet Nathan giving a story illustration to David so that he could see his own sins:

> *"The Lord sent Nathan to David. When he came to him, he said, 'There were two men in a certain town, one rich and the other poor. The rich man had a very large number of sheep and cattle, but the poor man had nothing except one little ewe lamb he had bought. He raised it, and it grew up with him and his children. It shared his food, drank from his cup and even slept in his arms. It was like a daughter to him. Now a traveler came to the rich man, but the rich man refrained from taking one of his own sheep or cattle to prepare a meal*

for the traveler who had come to him. Instead, he took the ewe lamb that belonged to the poor man and prepared it for the one who had come to him.' David burned with anger against the man and said to Nathan, 'As surely as the Lord lives, the man who did this must die! He must pay for that lamb four times over, because he did such a thing and had no pity.' Then Nathan said to David, 'You are the man! This is what the Lord, the God of Israel, says: "I anointed you king over Israel, and I delivered you from the hand of Saul. Why did you despise the word of the Lord by doing what is evil in his eyes? You struck down Uriah the Hittite with the sword and took his wife to be your own. You killed him with the sword of the Ammonites. Now, therefore, the sword will never depart from your house, because you despised me and took the wife of Uriah the Hittite to be your own."' Then David said to Nathan, 'I have sinned against the Lord.' Nathan replied, 'The Lord has taken away your sin. You are not going to die.'"
2 Samuel 12

There are a couple of things about David's story that I find interesting. The first is that David wasn't able to see his own sin until Nathan introduced it as someone else's sin. We are blind to our own sins and we need God's mercy to point it out to us so that we can repent.

The second point is that when confronted with his sin, David didn't waste any time and repented immediately. David is often called a man after God's own heart and it certainly isn't because of his tendency to dive into sin like everyone else. It's because he repented quickly, unlike the Pharisees and Jonah. David's sin was worse than the Pharisees' and Jonah's sins. David had blood on his hands and yet, David was the one who understood he sinned and that he needed God's forgiveness. We need to look to David as our example here and be quick to repent of our sins as well.

Effects of Forgetting We Need Forgiveness

These examples show us the negative effects of our pride. Here are three reasons that forgetting we need forgiveness is bad for us:

Reason #1: We don't repent.

We will explore repentance more in the next chapter, but I want to emphasize how crucial repentance is to our salvation. We don't receive salvation without repentance. When God calls us to Himself, He first calls us to repent. Jesus said, "Repent, for the kingdom of heaven is near" (Matthew 4:17). We prepare ourselves for Heaven by repenting of our sins here on earth.

Satan wants us to be filled with pride because then we are not looking for help. I don't write this to shame anyone, but in the hopes that we will see our need for God, our sin as offensive, and our need for Jesus's blood to wipe away our sins. We can see an example of this in addiction programs. The first step in addiction programs is to admit that there is a problem, and our first step in our Christian walk is to admit that we have sin and we need to be saved from it. We can't receive Jesus's righteousness without admitting that we need Jesus.

Reason #2: We don't see the sweetness of Jesus.

When we rely on ourselves for our own righteousness, Jesus doesn't seem sweet. Until we see the depth from which we have fallen, we can't see Jesus's love in our lives. There is a large difference between fear-based religion and having a relationship with a loving Savior. When Jesus is sweet, we live our days walking beside Him, in alignment with His will. When Jesus isn't sweet to us, we either disregard Him or react to Him out of fear rather than resting in Him.

We want to be Christians who are walking with our Savior, knowing fully that He is the reason we are saved from our sins and then able to do good works.

Reason #3: We aren't working for God's Glory:
We have already discussed that our primary purpose in this world is to glorify God with our lives. When we don't repent and rely on God to live our lives in a manner pleasing to Him, we misrepresent Him to the rest of the world. When people who claim Christianity don't admit their sins and repent, the rest of the world gets a distorted view of Jesus.

We saw already that we were created for good works (Ephesians 2:10), but we can't carry those out without God working them in our lives. We want to be people who are used by God for His glory!

HOW WE REMEMBER

How about you? Do you see your need for repentance and God's saving grace in your life? Ask God to help you see the depth of your sin and turn to Him for help. Do you compare yourself to others, thinking that you are "good" because maybe you haven't failed as much as other people? Tell yourself the truth from God's Word that no one is righteous, not even one (Romans 3:10).

I write this in hopes that we see the sweetness of Jesus. Jesus is sweet when we see that He laid down His life for ours and how He suffered so that we could be reconciled to God.

There are three ways you can respond to this information:

1. Pray these verses: "Search me, God, and know my heart; test me and know my anxious thoughts. See if there is any offensive way in me, and lead me in the way everlasting" (Psalm 139:23-24). This prayer helps renew our relationship with God. We can tether ourselves to Him by examining our inner life to see if there is anything offensive.
2. Put your faith in Jesus. If you have been reading this chapter and thinking that you haven't trusted in Jesus for the forgiveness of your sins, I pray that you would. We need to repent and tell God we are sorry for our sins and turn to Him to help us live our days in a manner pleasing to Him. We don't obey Him out of fear, but out of gratitude for our salvation. We live our days with faith that Jesus has taken our sins away at the cross and we are reconciled to God.
3. Live in a posture of humility, knowing that it isn't your own righteousness that saves, but Jesus's righteousness. We can imagine that our hands are open before the Lord and we are willing to walk in whatever way He wants us to.

Gospel Rhythm: Repentance

> *"It is not the absence of sin but the grieving over it which distinguishes the child of God from empty professors."*
> — A. W. Pink

Introduction

All stories of salvation begin with repentance. If we can't see that we need to be saved, we can't be saved. John Bunyan started his life as a very sinful boy. He cursed, lusted, and lived his life with a great deal of pride. He never felt God's conviction in his life; it seemed he had seared his conscience. Then one day he heard a sermon that convicted his soul: "Wherefore I fell in my Conscience under his Sermon, thinking and believing that he made that Sermon on purpose to show me my evil doing. And at that time I felt what guilt was, though never before, that I can remember."[11]

John Bunyan was convicted of his sin and brought to a place of repentance for the saving of his soul. God shows each of us mercy when He reveals our sinful states to us. When we see the weight of our sins, we can then come to Him for the help that we need. When we don't understand our great need for Jesus on the cross, we won't cling to Him as our Savior.

Being able to repent after we are convicted of sin is a beautiful gift from a loving Father. Most of us are familiar with the prodigal son parable in Luke 15. The younger son squandered his father's inheritance by delving deep into sinful living while the older son stayed home. After the inheritance ran out, the younger son found himself a job feeding pigs to keep from starving. As he longed to eat the food the pigs were eating, he thought he could go back to his father, not as a son, but as a hired hand. When the younger son came back, the father accepted him as a son and all was forgiven.

This is a beautiful picture of how God, our heavenly Father, welcomes us after we repent. God lovingly convicts us of our sin and harmful ways of living, and then allows us to draw near to Him again in repentance because Jesus paid the price for our sins. When we go to God in repentance, we are met with open arms the same way the prodigal son was met with his father's open arms.

Though conviction of sin doesn't always feel like a gift, I am grateful that God convicts me of my sin. Without the gift of conviction, I would never come to repent of the sins in my life. Without repenting of my sins, I wouldn't receive the righteousness of Jesus. I wouldn't receive the gift of being a child of God. When God convicts me of my sins, I don't treat it like a gift.

Often, I feel ashamed and embarrassed. I want to hide from God rather than approach Him with repentance. God lovingly guides me to repentance and I can walk in freedom once again, knowing that I am doing what I was born to do, glorify God.

In this chapter, we will discuss how crucial repentance is for our salvation, what repentance is, look at examples of Biblical repentance, and then end with how wonderful restoration with God after repentance is.

God's Instructions For Salvation

We saw in a previous chapter that the Bible tells one big story about God's plan to redeem His people. God had a plan from the beginning to bring His sinful people back to Him. Part of God's plan was to use John the Baptist to prepare the people for Jesus's coming. "In the beginning of the gospel about Jesus Christ, the Son of God. It is written in Isaiah the prophet: 'I will send my messenger ahead of you, who will prepare your way' — a voice of one calling in the desert, 'Prepare the way for the Lord, make straight paths for Him.' And so John came, baptizing in the desert region and preaching a baptism of repentance for the forgiveness of sins" (Mark 1:1-4).

God's message that He sent with John the Baptist was a message of repentance. In order for us to be ready for our Savior, we need to see the depth of our sin and repent. After John, Jesus began preaching repentance: "From that time on Jesus began to preach, "Repent, for the kingdom of heaven is near" (Matthew 4:17). After Jesus preached on repentance, Peter and Paul took up the mission of preaching repentance: "Peter said, 'Repent, then, and turn to God, so that your sins may be wiped out, that times of refreshing may come from the Lord, and that he may send the Messiah, who has been appointed for you—even Jesus. Heaven must receive him until the time comes for God to restore everything, as he promised long ago through his holy prophets'" (Acts 3:19-21). Paul said, "In the past God overlooked such ignorance, but now he commands all people everywhere to repent" (Acts 17:30). It is clear from these passages that God intends for His people to repent of their sins with faith in Jesus for forgiveness. Repentance with faith in Jesus is the way we can receive God's salvation.

The people of Isaiah's time received this message: "In repentance and rest is your salvation, in quietness and trust is your strength…" (Isaiah 30:15). We receive salvation by repenting of our sins and resting in God. When we repent, we can truly rest because we know that God has removed our sins and our lives are under His authority. We rest in the fact that He has saved us and we can depend on Him rather than ourselves. The Old Testament is filled with prompts to "Return, Israel, to the Lord your God. Your sins have been your downfall!" (Hosea 14:1). The Bible makes it clear that repentance is an important piece not only to our salvation (justification) but also to our ongoing relationship with God (sanctification).

When we first come to Jesus with repentance for the forgiveness of our sins, it will feel like a large weight has been removed from us. As we continue to go to Jesus with repentance, it might start to feel deflating that we continue to sin. The good news is that at first we are convicted of major sins that will have a major effect on our lives. As we continue our Christian walk, we will start to pinpoint more sins and attitudes that aren't pleasing to

God. They may not be blatant and obvious, but God helps us to continue to be refined our entire lives. We will continue to come to Him in repentance and continue to be refined into the people God intends for us to be.

I've heard sanctification compared with pulling weeds from the yard. The first weeds to go will be the biggest weeds. After the bigger weeds are pulled, then we can start to see the smaller weeds growing. These weeds weren't as noticeable before because the big weeds were blocking our vision. It is the same with our sin. When we come to Jesus for the forgiveness of our sins, the first sins that are removed are the blatant ones. After those sins are taken care of, we notice more and more the little sins that we have been hiding away behind the big ones. We will continue this process of removing sins our whole lives. No, the big ones won't continue, but we will continue to be convicted of small sins over and over again.

2 Peter 3:18 says: "The Lord is not slow in keeping his promise, as some understand slowness. Instead he is patient with you, not wanting anyone to perish, but everyone to come to repentance." God wants His children to know Him and to repent of their sins so that by grace through faith, they can receive the benefit of Jesus's sacrifice on the cross.

Repentance is a basic principle of the Christian faith. The author of Hebrews puts it this way: "Therefore let us leave the elementary teachings about Christ and go on to maturity, not laying again the foundation of repentance from acts that lead to death, and of faith in God, instruction and baptisms, the laying on of hands, the resurrection of the dead, and eternal judgment" (Hebrews 6:1). When we come to faith, repentance is a core element of Christianity. It is an elementary teaching that is necessary and not optional.

What is Repentance

The definition for repentance in English is: a. to feel regret or contrition or b. to change one's mind.[12] The Hebrew word for repentance means a return and in Greek it means a change of mind.[13] Repentance means to turn from our old way of living or to change our minds about how we have been living. We feel remorse for our sins and we turn a different direction toward Jesus. Paul explained repentance to the church in Rome succinctly: "God's kindness leads you toward repentance" (Romans 2:4). God is kind enough to reveal our sin to us and to allow us to turn away from it. Often when God reveals sin, it doesn't feel like kindness. It may feel like we are being shamed or picked on, but God isn't shaming or picking on us. He is giving us mercy to see our sin and the mess that it makes in our lives. He is giving us a chance to turn from it back toward Him.

God not only gives us commands, but He also gives us examples in His Word of people carrying out those commands. Paul wrote a letter to the people in Corinth to try and reconcile their relationship after Paul had rebuked them. These verses that Paul wrote to the Corinthians portray repentance well:

> *"Even if I caused you sorrow by my letter, I do not regret it. Though I did regret it—I see that my letter hurt you, but only for a little while— yet now I am happy, not because you were made sorry, but because your sorrow led you to repentance. For you became sorrowful as God intended and so were not harmed in any way by us. Godly sorrow brings repentance*

that leads to salvation and leaves no regret, but worldly sorrow brings death. See what this godly sorrow has produced in you: what earnestness, what eagerness to clear yourselves, what indignation, what alarm, what longing, what concern, what readiness to see justice done. At every point you have proved yourselves to be innocent in this matter."
2 Corinthians 7:9-11

The church at Corinth expressed sorrow for their sin and turned from it. Paul described it well when he talked of their earnestness and eagerness to clear themselves. When God convicts us of our sins, we want to make things right again. We don't want to hide and pretend we did no wrong, but rather, we want to admit our guilt and make things right again.

The worldly sorrow that Paul is referring to means embarrassment for getting caught, but godly sorrow helps kill the sin that tears us away from God. We want God to produce godly sorrow in us so that we can see our sin for what it is and turn away from it.

King David Repents

King David gives an excellent example of godly sorrow. We saw in the last chapter that King David fell deep into sin when he took another man's wife and then had him killed. Psalm 51 is a prayer from David after the prophet Nathan confronted him with his sin. It is a blessing that Psalm 51 is in the Bible because we all sin and this prayer of David gives us a framework to guide us as we move toward repentance.

I would like to explore three areas as we move through this Psalm:

1. David relied on God's strength instead of his own.

David started out begging for God's mercy: "Have mercy on me, O God, according to your unfailing love; according to your great compassion blot out my transgressions" (Psalm 51:1). David knew God's unfailing love and great compassion, and he recalls these attributes back to God. He was essentially saying, "God, I know you have unfailing love and I know you are compassionate."

David reminded himself of who God is as he begged for mercy. David could have given a list of his own strengths, saying, "I know that I sinned terribly in this scenario, but look at all the good I have done. I defeated Goliath, I am leading Israel as king, and I have been a mighty warrior for You in battle." David could have attempted to rest in his presumed strength, but that is not what God is asking for. David rested in God's character rather than his own.

"You do not delight in sacrifice, or I would bring it; you do not take pleasure in burnt offerings. The sacrifices of God are a broken spirit; a broken and contrite heart, O God, you will not despise" (Psalm 51:16-17). David knew that he couldn't achieve anything to receive God's forgiveness. God wants a heart that is humble and obedient to Him. Sacrifices could become mindless habits without having a heart that was truly repenting. God desires our hearts to be broken and willing to turn away from our sin in obedience.

2. David's example of repentance.

"Wash away all my iniquity and cleanse me from my sin" (Psalm 51:2). David's prayer teaches us what to ask God when we come to Him to repent. We want God to wash away our sins. We need cleansing.

"For I know my transgressions, and my sin is always before me. Against you, you only, have I sinned and done what is evil in your sight, so that you are proved right when you speak and justified when you judge. Surely I was sinful at birth, sinful from the time my mother conceived me. Surely you desire truth in the inner parts; you teach me wisdom in the inmost place. Cleanse me with hyssop, and I will be clean; wash me, and I will be whiter than snow" (Psalm 51:3-7). David admitted here that he is aware how terrible his sin is and yet he was calling on God to wash him clean.

When we repent, God restores us and gives us a clean conscience again. Our sins are removed and we don't need to feel guilt or shame over them any longer. We can stand before the Lord knowing that we are in right standing with Him. "Let me hear joy and gladness; let the bones you have crushed rejoice" (Psalm 51:8). "Restore to me the joy of your salvation and grant me a willing spirit to sustain me" (Psalm 51:12). There is joy when we know that Almighty God has forgiven us our sins. We can be light and not heavy-laden because our burdens have been lifted.

When we have a guilty conscience, we live lives with a paranoia that we will be caught. We live our days with anxiety and stress worrying about when our sins will be found out. When we are free from sin, we are truly free. We don't have to look over our shoulders in paranoia; we can live unhindered from the burden of guilt and worry.

3. David prayed for strength to resume glorifying God with his life.

The primary concern for Christians is the glory of God. When we become Christians, we stop thinking about our own interests and replace them with God's interests. David asked in this psalm to be reinstated to do good works for God's glory. "Then I will teach transgressors your ways, and sinners will turn back to you" (Psalm 51:13). "O Lord, open my lips, and my mouth will declare your praise" (Psalm 51:15). The prodigal son thought he would be a hired hand for his father, but his father reinstated him to sonship. We receive the same benefit when we are forgiven of our sins after we repent. We are children of God and we are free to obey and glorify Him with our lives.

Restoration With God

> "Blessed is he whose transgressions are forgiven, whose sins are covered. Blessed is the man whose sin the Lord does not count against him and in whose spirit is no deceit."
> Psalm 32:1-2

I have already communicated about my tendency towards pride. For the majority of my life, I have struggled to see my own sin and its negative effects on my life, as well as the lives of my loved ones. I am thankful that God mercifully showed me the depth of my sin and now I can say with David that I am blessed because my transgressions are forgiven. My sins are covered. I don't have to try and cover up my sin and guilt. Because of my repentant faith in Jesus, I know that I have been washed clean. I can live a truly free life.

> *"When I kept silent, my bones wasted away through my groaning all day long. For day and night Your hand was heavy upon me; my strength was sapped as in the heat of summer. Then I acknowledged my sin to you and did not cover up my iniquity. I said, 'I will confess my transgressions to the Lord' and You forgave the guilt of my sin."*
> Psalm 32:3-5

Can't you just feel the oppression of sin by David's words in this psalm? "My bones wasted away, I groaned all day long, your hand was heavy upon me;" there is pain and anguish in this psalm. Have you felt this pain and anguish in your own life? I know that I have. I have felt the oppression of my guilt and shame. I have felt like I can never escape the effects of my sin. It is a true gift to be able to come to God in repentance and that He forgives the guilt of our sins.

> *"Rejoice in the Lord and be glad, you righteous; sing, all you who are upright in heart!"*
> Psalm 32:11

God doesn't leave us in our sinful states. He mercifully rebukes us for our sins. God confronts our sin for our ultimate good. He is a loving Father who won't leave us in the deadly states we are in. He points out the futility of our sin and allows us to come to Him for those sins to be forgiven. I hope that we can all look at repentance as a gift rather than a hoop we have to jump through. Repentance is a gift from a loving Father that allows us to draw near to Him again.

HOW WE REMEMBER

Have you repented of your sins to receive God's gift of salvation through faith in Jesus? Do you confess your sins easily, or do you hold onto them? Is God your hiding place or do you hide from Him?

- Examine yourself and repent regularly as a gospel rhythm. Use Psalm 51 as your guide. Commit it to memory so it is there when you need it.

We Forget: We Are Forgiven

"There is no sin so great but that Jesus Christ is greater. There is no sin so much for which Jesus Christ did not die. There is no sin so deeply rooted in our nature but that Jesus Christ can pull it up by the roots." - Thomas Brooks

Introduction:

After having four children, I was unable to take my wedding ring off. It was stuck and I felt ashamed. I was embarrassed that my ring was stuck because it revealed that I had gained weight. I did what most people do when they feel shame: I hid. I didn't tell my husband Peter that my ring was stuck on my finger. I just pretended everything was fine. Eventually, I needed to get a medical procedure where I couldn't wear my ring. I had to face the facts and go get my ring cut off. As soon as the ring was cut off, I felt free. Not only my finger, which felt a lot better, but also my soul felt free. I had been harboring a secret from my husband that now was brought to the light. I wasn't hiding in shame anymore.

Shame is a common theme in this world. There is not one person who doesn't hold some sense of shame over sin in their lives or shame for feeling like they can't measure up. We beat ourselves up for past sins and we beat ourselves up for things that aren't sins but that our culture frowns upon. Many of us experience this guilt and shame and we try to cover and hide ourselves. We feel we are too far gone and will never be able to be forgiven, so we hide.

Martin Luther was a monk in the 16th Century. Luther struggled in his adult life with guilt and shame over his sin. He felt that he could never be good enough to earn God's favor. He would spend hours in the confessional, and when he emerged, he would feel a sense of pride. Then felt he needed to go back and confess his pride![16] This type of struggle is hard to watch and it certainly isn't what God intended for our lives. Yes, God does intend for us to repent of our sins continuously, but God also intends for us to rest in Jesus's work on the cross.

We can't feel God's love for us when we are hiding from Him. I also couldn't receive my husband's affirmation of love and care for me when I was pushing him away. When I told my husband about my ring, his response was compassion and love. When we ask God to forgive us for our sins, His response is compassion and love as well. We don't need to stay in the darkness, we can feel God's love in the light.

"But God demonstrates his own love for us in this:
While we were still sinners, Christ died for us."
Romans 5:8

True Guilt vs. False Guilt

Remember the Pharisees? They were notorious for laying a heavy load on the people of that day.

We do the same thing today. We take God's law and add to it, imposing a heavy burden on people that God never intended for us to follow. Many of our "cultural rules" revolve around appearance, performance, wealth, and health.

- Appearance—Our modern rules say that we need to look good. We need to have good-looking homes, yards, children, churches, and vehicles. We feel the need to have our homes spotless and to look good all the time.
- Performance—Our culture says that our worth is in how we perform.
- Wealth—We feel we need to do anything to attain wealth, even if that means getting it through unsavory means.
- Health—This area feels like a revolving door. Health trends are constantly changing and evolving. It is impossible and exhausting to keep up.

Do you feel guilt and shame for breaking these modern-day pharisaical laws? I know I do. How much time do you spend trying not to break these laws? Make no mistake, God cares about our appearance, performance, wealth, and health. He wants us to honor Him in every one of these areas. We should honor God with our lives, but we shouldn't be so concerned about what men might think. God's rules don't keep changing like our cultural rules do. God's concern is with the posture of our heart more than us looking good in the eyes of man. Paul warns the church in Galatia not to fear man: "Am I now trying to win the approval of human beings, or of God? Or am I trying to please people? If I were still trying to please people, I would not be a servant of Christ" (Galatians 1:10).

Part of our job as Christians is to distinguish between God's conviction and false guilt. God's conviction informs us when we have broken God's Law. We understand that we need to repent of our sins to be in a right relationship with God again. False guilt is feeling guilty not about breaking God's laws but about breaking an unwritten cultural law. The best way to discern God's conviction from false guilt is to know God's Word and make a habit of repenting when we feel convicted.

When we see that our guilt is from God's conviction in our lives, we thank God for His mercy in showing us our sin and allowing us to come to repentance. We repent and then we move forward in freedom because we know that we are forgiven. When we see that our guilt is false guilt, we ask God to help us to keep our eyes on Him and help us to know that we don't have to obey the world's standards. We are free to obey God. Ask God to show you what He wants with your days rather than striving after what the world says is pleasing.

Many times my sin has left me feeling truly convicted. There have been so many times where I have been really ugly to Peter during a disagreement or I lost my temper with my kids, and it sends me to a place of shame thinking that I am not worthy of being in God's presence or my family's presence. I am guessing you have felt this type of guilt, when you know your sin has caused damage. Thankfully, as we have already learned, God allows us to repent and be restored to a good relationship with Him again. There is no sin that we can commit that can separate us from God. Jesus paid the price for all of them. When we are convicted of sin, rather than hiding in shame, we repent knowing that our sins will be wiped clean.

I have also felt false guilt for not measuring up to the world's standards. I feel false guilt when the doorbell rings and the house isn't perfectly clean, when it's swimsuit season and I don't feel like my body measures up, or when I'm in the presence of someone who commands more attention than me. There are many ways to feel like I don't measure up in this world. In those times, I can pray to my heavenly Father, and He will show me who I am in Christ. I need to be grounded in God's Truth rather than the world's standards. I am sure that I will be susceptible to the world's false truths until God takes me home, but I can fight this wrongful thinking by staying in step with the Spirit. Staying in step with the Spirit (Galatians 5:25) means that we look to obey God in every aspect of our lives. We live our lives looking to Him for answers rather than trying to obey and please Him on our own.

Free to Obey

Jesus died on the cross for our sins. This means that they are taken away from us. Jesus endured the punishment for them already. We don't have to beat ourselves up about past sin and we certainly don't have to beat ourselves up about not reaching a cultural standard that isn't a sin. We are free to live shame-free lives. When we know that our sins are forgiven, the rightful response is gratitude. When we are grateful for the forgiveness of sins, we want to live our lives in a way that is pleasing to God.

The apostle Paul in his letter to the Romans addressed the difference between being a slave to sin and a slave to righteousness. We are slaves either way. One way leads to death, the other to life. If we are slaves to sin, we are stuck in pits that will hurt and destroy our lives. Being a slave to righteousness is much different, being a slave to the best Master. We are free to obey God and we know that obeying His Word leads to full satisfaction in this life and the next one.

> *"I am using an example from everyday life because of your human limitations. Just as you used to offer yourselves as slaves to impurity and to ever-increasing wickedness, so now offer yourselves as slaves to righteousness leading to holiness. When you were slaves to sin, you were free from the control of righteousness. What benefit did you reap at that time from the things you are now ashamed of? Those things result in death! But now that you have been set free from sin and have become slaves of God, the benefit you reap leads to holiness, and the result is eternal life. For the wages of sin is death, but the gift of God is eternal life in Christ Jesus our Lord."*
> Romans 6:19-23

Paul also teaches the church in Corinth that after we are justified in Christ, our old sinful self is no longer living. It is put to death. When someone is a Christian, they are able to be Christ's ambassadors. We can live joyful lives sharing this good news with others so they may take part in the removal of their sins.

> *"Therefore, if anyone is in Christ, he is a new creation; the old has gone, the new has come! All of this is from God, who reconciled us to Himself through Christ and gave us the ministry of reconciliation: that God was reconciling the world to*

> *Himself in Christ, not counting men's sins against them. And He has committed to us the message of reconciliation. We are therefore Christ's ambassadors, as though God were making His appeal through us. We implore you on Christ's behalf: Be reconciled to God! God made Him who had no sin to be sin for us, so that in Him we might become the righteousness of God."*
> 2 Corinthians 5:17-21

What a joy it is that we get to be Christ's ambassadors. We get to represent Him to the world. We are a new creation! Now we can proceed in our lives with the purpose of glorifying God! Our joy is made complete when we walk in freedom by obeying Him.

Future Hope

Forgiveness for sins frees us up to glorify God with our lives here on earth, but we also have a future hope to look forward to. The apostle Peter tells Christians who have been scattered because of religious persecution:

> *"Praise be to the God and Father of our Lord Jesus Christ! In his great mercy he has given us new birth into a living hope through the resurrection of Jesus Christ from the dead, and into an inheritance that can never perish, spoil or fade. This inheritance is kept in heaven for you, who through faith are shielded by God's power until the coming of the salvation that is ready to be revealed in the last time. In all this you greatly rejoice, though now for a little while you may have had to suffer grief in all kinds of trials."*
> 1 Peter 1:3-6

We have a future hope in Heaven, where there will be no more sorrow, pain, and trials in this life. While we live on earth, we can live grateful lives to God, not lives of guilt and shame. We can also look forward to our future inheritance, where we will see God's face and won't have to struggle against sin in this world.

When we keep our eyes focused on Jesus and the future hope that He promises us, the world won't have a hold on us. We won't get lost trying to be okay in this world. Looking to Jesus helps us set our priorities, knowing that no matter what happens in this world, we are going to inherit eternal life. Looking to our future hope helps us not to get sucked into the ways of the world.

Jesus Reinstates Peter

Our guilt over sin can cause us to run away from God, but in His mercy, God allows us to repent and continue to glorify Him with our lives. Jesus gives an example of this forgiveness when He reinstated Peter. Peter denied Jesus three times in Jesus's darkest hour before He went to the cross. I can imagine Peter spent plenty of time beating himself up over this collapse. After Jesus rose from the dead and before He ascended into heaven, Jesus made sure to care for Peter's soul:

> *"When they had finished eating, Jesus said to Simon Peter, 'Simon son of John, do you love me more than these?'*
>
> *'Yes, Lord,' he said, 'you know that I love you.'*
> *Jesus said, 'Feed my lambs.'*
> *Again Jesus said, 'Simon son of John, do you love me?'*
> *He answered, 'Yes, Lord, you know that I love you.'*
> *Jesus said, 'Take care of my sheep.'*

> *The third time he said to him, 'Simon son of John, do you love me?'*
>
> *Peter was hurt because Jesus asked him the third time, 'Do you love me?' He said, 'Lord, you know all things; you know that I love you.' Jesus said, 'Feed my sheep.'"*
>
> John 21:15-17

Jesus asks Peter three times because Peter denied Jesus three times. Jesus also gave Peter a job to do. We are happiest when we are able to contribute to God's Kingdom. Jesus was telling Peter to be free from his guilt and shame, and move on to taking care of Jesus's lambs. When we are walking in freedom from the forgiveness of our sins, we will be doing good works for God's Kingdom. These good works don't come from trying to earn forgiveness, they are out of gratitude for the forgiveness we have received.

In Jesus, we don't have to live in guilt and shame of our sin. Jesus serves as our mediator and we know that our sins are removed as far as the east is from the west (Psalm 103:12).

When We Get Stuck

Sometimes we can still get stuck in a pattern of guilt and shame. We are rendered useless for God's Kingdom work when we beat ourselves up for sins that are forgiven. We can also start to feel unworthy of doing God's work. We worry that our motives aren't pure and we get stuck.

We first need to remember that:

> *"There is now no condemnation for those who are in Christ Jesus."*
>
> Romans 8:1

And secondly, Andrew Peterson made a good point on the Journeywomen podcast:

> *"The best thing you can do is to remember that God is going to redeem your screw-ups. That's what he does. That takes the pressure off. Your motives are never going to be perfectly pure. One of the worst things that can happen is that you can be so worried about whether you're doing it for the right reasons that you do nothing at all."*[13]

Satan would love nothing more than us getting stuck in our sin and shame. He wants us to feel like we can't come back to God because of our sin. Adam and Eve sinned and God clothed them and took care of them. The Israelites complained after God miraculously led them out of Egypt by parting the Red Sea and God brought them to the promised land. Gideon asked for a sign over and over in disbelief, and God gave Gideon victory as well as a sign. Both King David and the apostle Paul were involved in murder, and they were both used mightily for God's Kingdom.

God is a God of restoration and forgiveness. When we come to Him with repentant hearts, on the basis of Christ's substitutionary sacrifice of atonement on the cross, He is sure to forgive the most egregious offense. God is loving and merciful and we can trust Him to care for us both in this life and the next.

We will all feel guilt and shame at different times. Remember that our righteousness is in Jesus, not from ourselves. No matter how far you may have fallen, you are not too far from God's love and forgiveness. You just need to ask for it.

HOW WE REMEMBER

Do you struggle with false guilt in your life? Do you run away from God rather than come to Him in repentance?

1. Ask God for help to discern between God's conviction and false guilt. Repent when you feel conviction and ask God to help you lean into Him when you feel false guilt.
2. If you are struggling to believe that you are forgiven, you can imagine Jesus on the cross. Christ paid the penalty that our sins deserve. The more we look to Him, the more we see His righteousness rather than our sins.
3. Ask God each day how you can be His ambassador, using your freedom from sin to obey Him in gratitude with the strength that He provides. Pray throughout your days and help God discern what He wants you to do.

Gospel Rhythm: Prayer

> *"The first great and primary business to which I ought to attend every day is to have my soul happy in the Lord."*
> *- George Muller*

Introduction

Prayer can be a loaded topic. Often I think the experience can be heavy with guilt. We feel guilty because we think that we haven't prayed enough, or for the right things, or in the right way. In my own experience, if I haven't been praying frequently, I feel the need to hide from God because I worry that I have disappointed Him. But God isn't sitting in Heaven with His arms crossed, angry that I haven't come to Him. The truth is that prayer is a gift to me. I am the one missing out on sweet communion with God. Prayer isn't another item on my to-do list, it is an invitation to get my cup filled by my Creator! When I stop thinking of God being disappointed with me for not coming to Him enough and start thinking about how He fills me when I pray, I will come running to communion with

God far more frequently than I will out of a sense of duty or obligation.

Think about your closest relationships. You are close to those people because you interact with them. You share yourself with these people. They know your likes/dislikes, your fears, and your joys. God knows these things about you also, but He enjoys hearing them from you. He loves to commune with you in a relationship. When we stop talking to the people closest to us, our relationships suffer. When we stop talking to God, our relationship with Him suffers as well.

It is encouraging to remember that He is there no matter what we are going through. Once, our family was vacationing in the Great Smoky Mountains and our cabin was on a steep mountain road. As we were trying to navigate our way to the cabin for the first time, we pulled into the wrong driveway. We had to make a three-point turn on a very steep incline and we were all pretty scared. I looked in the back and told the kids to pray and from the back, our oldest daughter said, "I already am." What a joy for my mother's heart that she was drawing near to God in her time of fear. Thankfully we were able to make the turn and get to our cabin's driveway without any mishaps.

Prayer is a gift and a reward that God gives us while we walk in joy and pain and in everything in between. I would like to outline a method of prayer in this chapter that I heard in a sermon. This method has become a staple in my life. This method uses the acronym of P.R.A.Y.[14]

"P" is for Praise

The P in the P.R.A.Y. acronym stands for praise. We start by praising God because He is worthy of all our praise. When we praise God for who He is and His character, we are in our rightful place, and God is in His. Remember that God made us to glorify Him. We should start our prayers by doing just that. Scripture is filled to the brim with verses that praise God for who He is and what He has done for us. We can pray these verses back to God.

> "Your ways, God, are holy. What god is as great as our God?
> You are the God who performs miracles;
> You display Your power among the peoples."
> Psalm 77:13-14

> "Great are the works of the Lord;
> they are pondered by all who delight in them.
> Glorious and majestic are his deeds,
> and his righteousness endures forever.
> He has caused his wonders to be remembered;
> the Lord is gracious and compassionate.
> He provides food for those who fear him;
> He remembers his covenant forever."
> Psalm 111:2-5

These verses are examples of what I have used in the praise section in my prayer journal. What has helped me immensely is having Bible verses highlighted in green from my Bible reading time about God's character. They are easy to pick out, making it easy for me to praise God with His Word. There are many hymns of praise to God as well. Play a hymn and just meditate on the lyrics, thanking God for who He is.

This section was the hardest for me when I started using the P.R.A.Y. method. I had a hard time coming up with what to say, but I found that the more I see God's character in Scripture or meditate on His character in songs, the more my heart wants to praise God.

"R" is for Repent
The R in the P.R.A.Y. acronym stands for repent. We have already covered repentance, but it is important that we repent after we praise God during our prayers. This acknowledges that we are sinful and we need God's help. We need Jesus's forgiveness. This section of prayer allows God to search our hearts and it helps to restore us to a right relationship with Him again. We will need to repent over the course of our entire lives. Just as Christian would get off the path in *Pilgrim's Progress*, we get off the path and need to be restored. Repentance is God's way of restoring us again.

When I come before the Lord and ask Him to search my heart, He usually shows me where I am straying from His plan for my life. Having repentance as a staple in my life gives me confidence that I am following God and the path He intends for my life. I know when I haven't made a habit of repentance because I feel bogged down in guilt, or my affections are chasing something other than God. It is good when my conscience is clean because I have laid it before the Lord.

"A" is for Ask
The A in the P.R.A.Y acronym stands for ask. This is where we ask God for our needs and the needs of our loved ones. When we put the ask category underneath praise and repentance, it

prevents us from going to God like He's a vending machine or a magic genie. We remind ourselves who He is, and who we are in relation to Him, and then we come before Him with our requests.

When we understand God's Word, we will have the discernment to know what prayers are pleasing to God. God's Word even commands us to pray for: everyone (1 Timothy 2:1), other believers (Ephesians 3:16), those who persecute us (Matthew 5:44), and our leaders (1 Timothy 2:1-3).

We should pray for things that are pleasing to God, such as His will being done on earth (Matthew 6:10), that God would save unbelievers (Romans 10:1), that God would give us what we need to do His will (Matthew 6:11), that God would send many people to do His work (Matthew 9:38), and for help from trouble and for healing (James 5:13-16). This is not an exhaustive list, but it helps to know who and what we can be praying for when we are asking God for help.

"Y" is for Yield
The Y in the acronym P.R.A.Y. stands for yield. This part of prayer is all about surrendering and acknowledging that God is sovereign over our entire lives, submitting to God's will in our lives. Just as Jesus prayed in the Lord's Prayer: "Our Father in heaven, hallowed be your name, your kingdom come, your will be done, on earth as it is in heaven" (Matthew 6:9). We want our lives yielded to God's will, even if that means He answers our prayers with a no. God ultimately knows and will give us what is best for us. This part of the prayer allows us to open-handedly trust God with everything we have.

Jesus Prays and Teaches About Prayer

I am so thankful that Jesus walked as a man on this earth, not only because He needed to in order for my sins to be forgiven, but because we have a model for what we should strive to be like. Jesus was a man of prayer and He depended on God as He walked the earth. Below are examples of Jesus showing us His dependence on God and modeling that we should depend on Him as well:

1. In times of grief. Jesus mourned the death of John the Baptist and retreated to a quiet place to pray (Matthew 14:13, 23). Jesus shows us that in times of deep sorrow, we can go to God in prayer. Though what is happening may feel terrible, we have a solid foundation that we can run to.

   The Psalms have many wonderful examples of lament, which is a prayer of deep sorrow. Lament is a way for us to pour out our hearts to God and tell Him what our true feelings are. I have often shied away from lamenting because I worry that I am insulting God or sinning by bringing my negative feelings to Him. I especially have a hard time when I have negative feelings about Him. Many of the Psalms of lament begin with telling God about hard emotional turmoil and then end by telling God attributes about Himself. When we follow this pattern, we can admit that living in this world is difficult and then be reminded that God is in control of it all. He is faithful.

2. When there is much work to do. While Jesus was staying in Capernaum, people brought Him all the sick

and demon-possessed (Mark 1:32). "Very early in the morning, while it was still dark, Jesus got up, left the house and went off to a solitary place, where he prayed" (Mark 1:35). Jesus was going to take His disciples to a quiet place but the crowds found Him. After feeding the crowds, Jesus took some time to pray (Mark 6:46). Jesus models for us a life that is dependent on God. Before we go to the work of daily living, we need to be filled with God. We will be ineffective if we try to do God's work on our own.

3. When there are crowds. Jesus was famous and many people wanted to see what Jesus was like. "Yet the news about him spread all the more, so that crowds of people came to hear him and to be healed of their sicknesses. But Jesus often withdrew to lonely places and prayed" (Luke 5:15-16). "Jesus, knowing that they intended to come and make him king by force, withdrew again to a mountain by himself" (John 6:15). Jesus advises us to be alone with God by how He lived His life. We need to have a personal relationship with God as well as a corporate relationship with God. We need time alone with Him.

4. Before Big Decisions. Jesus spent the night praying on a mountainside before He picked His disciples (Luke 6:12-13). Jesus modeled dependency on God the Father for His decision-making process. Jesus moved when God told Him to move. We should be in prayer about all of our decisions, the big and the small.

5. When We Don't Feel Up for the Task that Lies Ahead. When Jesus knew He was about to fulfill His duty on

the cross, He went to the Father for help: "Jesus went out as usual to the Mount of Olives, and His disciples followed him. On reaching the place, He said to them, 'Pray that you will not fall into temptation.' He withdrew about a stone's throw beyond them, knelt down and prayed, 'Father, if you are willing, take this cup from me; yet not my will, but yours be done.' An angel from heaven appeared to him and strengthened him. And being in anguish, he prayed more earnestly, and his sweat was like drops of blood falling to the ground" (Luke 22:39-44). Since we aren't bearing the sins of the world upon ourselves, all of our anguish and suffering pale in comparison to the suffering that Jesus endured on our behalf. We will face tasks that make us feel inadequate and will remind us that we need God. It is a gift to us that we can pray and ask God for help.

Jesus modeled prayer very regularly. Jesus also modeled a posture of humility and submission in His prayers. Some of his most famous prayers are The Lord's Prayer and His prayer in John 17. Jesus's life shows that prayer is important. Prayer is a primary means of connecting to God. Prayer is God's gift to us so that we can praise Him, get into proper relationship with Him, humbly rely on Him, and submit to His sovereign authority.

When You Don't Feel Like Praying
In this world, our motivations and desires for gospel rhythms like prayer ebb and flow. Sometimes, we feel really close to God and desire to pray regularly. Other times, prayer is more of a challenge. We may have a hard time connecting to God or even

concentrating on what we are praying. The answer in both of these cases is to keep going. Keep praying. God will meet you there.

Often when we think of prayer we think of sitting quietly with folded hands. I wanted to give some examples of different ways of praying when your prayer life needs to be revitalized.

- *Journaling* - Writing out prayer is a great way to keep your mind engaged in communicating with God. It also provides a reminder of what God has done in your life when you go back and read previous prayers.
- *Praying Out Loud*—If you are in a setting where you are able, praying out loud is a great way to keep your mind focused on God. Praying this way can make it feel more like chatting with a friend, and it can help prevent your mind from wandering during prayer.
- *Praying the Scripture* - As you are reading God's Word, the Holy Spirit will convict you of sin, encourage you, teach you, and challenge you. When you are convicted, you can ask God to forgive you. When you are encouraged, you can praise God and thank Him for the encouragement He brings. When you learn something new in Scripture, you can thank God for helping you to grow and ask Him to lead you as you continue on your journey. When you are challenged, you can ask God for help knowing that He is with us in everything that we do.
- *Worry Box*—Write down what you are worried about and put them away in a box or a place where they are all together. You can pray through each worry and then

put it away, and as you do, think of it as you are putting it out of your mind as well. They are put away, and they are in God's hands. You don't have to keep worrying about them.
- *Praying on Knees* - Praying on your knees puts you in the position you need to be with God. We know that our lives are to be lived in submission to Him. Praying this way can focus our minds on Him rather than on everything going on around us.

George Muller

George Muller was a man of great faith and prayer. He lived from 1805-1898 in Europe and his life was characterized by a deep dependence on God and prayer. He ran an orphanage and refused to ask for help or make their needs public. He didn't even collect a salary! The orphanage was run on prayers. One morning, the children were sitting at a table with no breakfast. George prayed and thanked God for the meal that wasn't there. Soon enough, the milkman showed up and asked them if they could use some milk because his cart had broken down. They were also provided with bread from the baker who woke up early that morning with an urgent prodding from God to bake bread for the orphanage.[17]

George Muller was a man who consistently relied on God for all of his needs. He trusted, and his faith grew because he believed that God would take care of him. George would take every burden to the Lord. Nearly all of his decisions were weighed in prayer. What a challenge to all of us. I have a tendency to get caught up in all the things of this physical world without remembering that I have a heavenly Father who is holding the whole world in His hands. George Muller inspires me to take everything to the Lord first.

Pray Without Ceasing

Jesus tells His disciples two parables about how we should be in persistent prayer:

> "Then Jesus said to them, 'Suppose you have a friend, and you go to him at midnight and say, "Friend, lend me three loaves of bread; a friend of mine on a journey has come to me, and I have no food to offer him." And suppose the one inside answers, "Don't bother me. The door is already locked, and my children and I are in bed. I can't get up and give you anything." I tell you, even though he will not get up and give you the bread because of friendship, yet because of your shameless audacity he will surely get up and give you as much as you need.'"
> Luke 11:5-8

This parable tells us to be persistent in prayer. God loves to hear from us and He is teaching us here that we should go to Him over and over and over again, to the point of annoyance. This may annoy mere mortals, but God loves for us to persist in prayer.

> "So I say to you: Ask and it will be given to you; seek and you will find; knock and the door will be opened to you. For everyone who asks receives; the one who seeks finds; and to the one who knocks, the door will be opened. Which of you fathers, if your son asks for a fish, will give him a snake instead? Or if he asks for an egg, will give him a scorpion? If you then, though you are evil, know how to give good gifts to your children, how much more will your Father in heaven give the Holy Spirit to those who ask him!"
> Luke 11:8-13

God is our heavenly Father and He loves to hear from His children. Our prayers may go unanswered but God will give us what we need from His loving hand. God loves us more than our earthly fathers who can only love us imperfectly. We go to our heavenly Father and ask.

What a gift that we can return to God again and again. He is there to listen to us. There will be times when He answers our prayers specifically, and there will be other times when He calms our hearts and allows us to let go of whatever we think we need. God discerns properly. He knows everything we need, and He will make sure we have what is right. He cares for us so we can go to Him with everything.

George Muller suggested that we begin each morning getting our hearts happy in the Lord. When I follow that advice, I find that I am living the way I was created to live. I would love to report to you that I am a great prayer warrior who gets up with the sun every morning and pours my heart out to the Lord. No, my prayer life often looks like diving into my day headfirst and then being reminded that I need God. I often have to go back to prayer, repent, and ask God to reorient my heart differently so I can serve Him in my day. When I start my day getting my heart happy in the Lord, I don't suffer from as much forgetfulness. I remember that God is in charge of the whole world, that I have a purpose for my day to serve and glorify Him, and that He will be with me in whatever I am facing that day. Prayer is a great reminder that God is Lord of all and helps me reorient my thoughts and actions around Him.

HOW WE REMEMBER

How comfortable are you in your prayer life? Do you feel like God is angry with you for not praying enough? Do you feel like you can approach the throne boldly?

Here are some helps for prayer:

1. I have been using a prayer journal from Val Marie Paper[18] for the last few years. I have enjoyed the prompts, the section to record thankfulness, and the section to write out my prayers. I always love looking back at where my spiritual journey has taken me.
2. If you are stuck in your prayer life you can try the P.R.A.Y. method, praying out loud, or praying on your knees. Whatever you try, know that God loves to hear from you and talking to Him will fill your cup to overflowing.

We Forget: In This World We Will Have Trouble

> *"He has chosen not to heal me, but to hold me. The more intense the pain, the closer his embrace."*
> *- Joni Eareckson Tada*

Introduction

"I wish that hadn't happened" is a thought that runs through my mind on a regular basis. Throughout my life, I have endured various hurts inflicted by both loved ones and acquaintances. We have all felt the sting of suffering to various degrees in our lives. The loss of loved ones, a child having to endure a disability, poverty, lack of people in your corner, and the list goes on. We can all remember situations where we have suffered.

Admittedly, I haven't suffered in my life nearly as much as others have. I also understand that won't always be the case. I have personally felt the sting of the death of loved ones, but most of my suffering has been more the nuisances of life: the busyness of motherhood and homeschooling, constantly feeling like I will never be "enough," and just feeling overwhelmed with the weight of the world.

There is a harmful idea permeating our culture called the prosperity gospel. This idea tells us that if we believe in God, we will prosper and never suffer. The prosperity gospel is a harmful idea to accept because we can start to doubt God's goodness when we face the trials of this life. Rather than believing God is allowing hard circumstances for our good, we get angry with Him because we feel entitled to an easy life. In this chapter, I want to highlight Christians who walked through hard trials and remained faithful to God knowing that God doesn't promise us ease and comfort here on earth.

Jesus tells us:

"I have told you these things, so that in me you may have peace. In this world you will have trouble. But take heart! I have overcome the world."
John 16:33

The apostle Peter encouraged the early church:

"Dear friends, do not be surprised at the fiery ordeal that has come on you to test you, as though something strange were happening to you."
1 Peter 4:12

Both Jesus and Peter were warning us that we won't get through this world unscathed. Pain and suffering will touch all of our lives. The good news is that Jesus has overcome sin and all of its effects, including death. When we put our hope and faith in Him, we can endure trials and hardships because we know that we are in His hands. I am always amazed when someone faces a terminal diagnosis with joy rather than bitterness, or when someone handles a disability with a good attitude that abides in Jesus rather than anger. Even though we think we are entitled to anger or a bad attitude in the midst of difficulty, God has a better way for us. He wants us to trust Him even in our suffering because He is our source of joy.

In This World, We Will Have Trouble

Suffering is experiencing pain of various kinds. We can suffer physically, relationally, emotionally, mentally, and spiritually.

My body suffers physically because I have celiac disease. I don't get to enjoy tasty foods made with gluten anymore because it will hurt my body. Diseases like celiac and even more severe diseases like cancer are a result of the fall. We weren't meant to have bodies that are susceptible to disease. When sin entered the world, our bodies started deteriorating on their way to eventual death. We will be under the curse of sin until we get to Heaven.

Suffering relationally may be one of the deepest forms of suffering. Not being able to connect with loved ones and having rifts in families and friendships is a hard road for many people. Misunderstandings and tunnel vision are common, and those wounds can cut deep. God intended for us to love each other as we ultimately love Him, but sin gets in the way of many of our deepest relationships. We also relationally suffer because of death. When our loved ones die, we are separated from them, and that hurts.

Emotional and mental suffering happens when our emotions and inner thoughts get the best of us. I suffer in this way when I can't separate reality from my perspective. I can start to believe negative ideas about myself and that my loved ones also believe these negative ideas. Mind games are hard to overcome and they also are a result of sin. It would be nice if we could always know the truth and believe it in our minds. We were meant to live in harmony and good relationships with each other and with God, but sin has tainted our relationships as well.

Spiritual suffering happens when we don't sense God's presence in our lives. I have felt this kind of suffering a few times in my life. There have been times when I have been praying, reading my Bible, and doing all the "right things," but I have a hard time feeling God's presence active in my life. Each time, God has mercifully brought me out by lighting a spark in my heart again to remind me that He is with me and He never left me. Though I know that He never left my side, it felt very hard and terrible when I couldn't sense Him near.

We will more than likely suffer in all of these categories over our lifetimes. When we trust in Jesus for the forgiveness of our sins, we have hope that we will not endure suffering in eternity. We are forgiven of our sins, and we will be with God forever, where there will be no more pain and suffering. Even though we are trusting in Jesus now, we need to be prepared to suffer, knowing that in the end, Jesus wins, and we will feel no more pain.

Why We Suffer

Let's take a quick look at three reasons why we suffer: 1. because of our own sin, 2. because of others' sin, and 3. because we are Christians.

1. We suffer because of our own sin.

We are all born with a sin nature and we all receive the effects of that nature. We can suffer physically, relationally, emotionally, mentally, and spiritually because of our own sin. Peter tells us in his first letter: "If you suffer, it should not be as a murderer or thief or any kind of criminal, or even as a meddler" (1 Peter 4:15). There are negative consequences to our sinful behavior. Peter is encouraging the believers scattered throughout Asia to: "Rid yourselves of all malice and all deceit, hypocrisy, envy, and slander of every kind. Like newborn babies, crave pure spiritual milk, so that by it you may grow up in your salvation, now that you have tasted that the Lord is good" (1 Peter 2:1-2). We see that we can suffer because of our sin and we should wage war with our sin so that we can glorify God. We don't want to suffer because of our poor choices and rebellion against God.

2. We suffer because of others' sins.

Unfortunately, we can also suffer in this world because of other people's sins. Sometimes we face suffering as a result of someone else's poor choices and rebellion against God. This can look like a child having to decide which parent to live with because the parents can't get along in a nasty divorce, or spouses who are hurt when their husband or wife sins or breaks a promise. We are affected by the sin of the people we are in closest relationships with.

This type of suffering can hurt. I have experienced this type of suffering in my life as I am sure that you have as well. The good news in this is that God can use these situations to bring us closer to Him and show us His love and comfort. It has a purpose.

There are also negative effects of living in a natural world that has been cursed by sin. Our physical bodies will wear out and die. There are terrible storms like tornadoes, hurricanes, tsunamis, and earthquakes that kill and injure many people at a time. One day, Christ will return and make all things new—but for now, the natural world shows us the effects of the fall and sin in general.

3. We suffer because we are Christians.

The last way we suffer is because we are Christians. The world is not a hospitable place for God's children. Satan prowls around this world looking for people that he can devour (1 Peter 5:8). We see in Isaiah 53 that Jesus suffered:

> *"He was despised and rejected by mankind, a man of suffering, and familiar with pain. Like one from whom people hide their faces he was despised, and we held him in low esteem. Surely he took up our pain and bore our suffering, yet we considered him punished by God, stricken by him, and afflicted."*
> Isaiah 53:3-4

We also see that because Jesus suffered, we will also. "The student is not above the teacher, nor a servant above his master" (Matthew 10:24). Jesus was giving His disciples advice before He sent them out. They needed to know that because Jesus suffered, they would too.

The disciples took this to heart after they were persecuted:

> *"The apostles left the Sanhedrin, rejoicing because they had been counted worthy of suffering disgrace for the Name."*
> Acts 5:41

The apostles were happy to suffer for the name of Jesus knowing that He also suffered while in the body. They knew that they were not above their teacher, but must also suffer while they were here on earth.

After Peter told the Christians scattered throughout Asia that they shouldn't suffer for their own sins, he encouraged them: "However, if you suffer as a Christian, do not be ashamed, but praise God that you bear that name" (1 Peter 4:16). We will suffer for being Christians, but we can praise God that we are chosen into His family.

We know that we will suffer in this world. If we're going to suffer, it is better to suffer for imitating Jesus than to suffer as a consequence of our sin. "For it is better, if it is God's will, to suffer for doing good than for doing evil" (1 Peter 3:17).

Suffering Has a Purpose

God allows us to suffer because 1. He draws us closer to Him in our suffering, 2. Our faith is proved genuine through our suffering, and 3. We can live lives that show the love of Jesus.

God Draws Us Closer to Him in Our Suffering

Suffering can work as an accelerant for our faith. Many times, suffering can shake us out of our sleepy walks of faith and produce good fruit in us. Suffering has a way of raising our eyes to God and His glory rather than looking around at the perceived treasures of this world. When we look through the perspectives of pain and suffering, we can more clearly see our dependence on God.

Idolatry has been a major issue for people throughout history. Though we don't worship golden statues like many people did in Bible times, we have our own forms of idolatry that we put in front of God. Sometimes our suffering may be a direct result of God removing an idol from our lives. Maybe God is removing our health, or the health of a loved one, or decreasing the amount of money in our bank account, or not allowing us to have the success we were hoping to have as a gracious act of love in order to redirect our attention and dependence back to Him. The removal of good gifts can feel very painful.

The futility of idolatry can be exposed within the midst of suffering. If a family member just received a terminal diagnosis, then does it really matter what number the scale says when you step on it? When suffering comes, does it matter how much money is in your bank account, if you wear name-brand clothing, if your house is the cleanest house on the block, or if you drive the newest model vehicle? Suffering gives us a clearer picture of what is important and what is not.

Suffering not only opens our eyes to the idols we have been clinging to, but it also reminds us that we are not in control of anything. Charles Spurgeon is attributed with saying: "I have learned to kiss the wave that throws me against the Rock of Ages."[21] It is a good thing for us to be thrown against the Rock of Ages. It is good for us to be reminded that we need to depend on God. Though suffering is not what we would ever ask for, it can bring us closer to God. Isn't closeness with God what is best for us? This isn't to say that evil is good, but that God uses even the hardships of this life to bring us closer to His heart.

As Christians, we will suffer, but not without purpose. God graciously uses our sufferings to help us depend on Him and cast aside the things of this world we had been clinging to. God uses suffering to show us with fresh eyes the way we should go.

Our Faith is Proved Genuine
One of the effects of prosperity on our church culture is nominal Christianity. A nominal faith means it is faith in name only. We go through the motions, but we don't live our lives passionately following Jesus. We live in a culture where we have everything at our fingertips, which allows us to live under the delusion that we are capable of providing for ourselves. When professing Christians live the same way as everyone else, seeming to not need God in their lives, Jesus isn't sweet. But when Christians live lives of risk, endure suffering and depend on Jesus for it, His name is glorified.

Peter tells the Christians in his first letter: *"For a little while you may have had to suffer grief in all kinds of trials. These have come so that your faith—of greater worth than gold, which perishes even though refined by fire—may be proved genuine and may result in praise, glory and honor when Christ Jesus is revealed"* (1 Peter 1:6-7).

Our faith is proven genuine when we suffer with joy clinging to Jesus.

Live Lives in Such a Way as to Show Others the Love of Jesus
The final purpose for suffering is to show a watching world Jesus's love for us. There is power in the testimony of those who have walked through suffering with grace and the peace of God. Peter instructs again: "Live such good lives among the pagans that, though they accuse you of doing wrong, they may see your good deeds and glorify God on the day He visits us" (1 Peter 2:12). One of our goals as Christians is to share God's love with those who don't know Him as their Lord and Savior. We want

to live lives that attract others to Jesus. When Christians endure suffering with hope and joy, it makes people curious, and following Jesus is appealing.

Tim Challies is a Christian author and blogger who experienced his deepest suffering to date with the loss of his 20-year-old son in 2020. His son was playing a game with his fiance, sister, and other college students when he collapsed. He never regained consciousness. Tim shared some of his feelings about it on his blog and I thought what he wrote was incredibly profound:

> "I have accepted suffering as something God has given me in sacred trust. Like talents and time and money and everything else God sovereignly bestows, I believe it can be stewarded faithfully or poorly. It's my intention to steward it well, for I'm convinced I'm responsible for it and accountable in it. It's my intention to be a faithful steward of this divine providence, this divine mystery, this divine gift. It's my great desire to someday hear, even in this, 'Well done good and faithful servant.' It's my longing to bow under it, to be shaped by it, to grow through it, and, by God's grace, to follow it on to new love and better service."
> -Tim Challies[18]

Tim's perspective on suffering is inspiring and helps us to see God's glory even over suffering.

Richard Wurmbrand is another wonderful example of depending on God in the face of great suffering. Richard was from Romania. He grew up Jewish but converted to Christianity and became a minister during a very dangerous time in Romania under Communist control. In 1948 he was imprisoned for his faith. He suffered much in his imprisonment. He was beaten and tortured and put in solitary confinement, but was still able to glorify God with his life. Jesus was with Richard in his imprisonment and Jesus is with us no matter what hardships we face.

Richard recalls preaching to the other prisoners in his confinement:

> *"It was strictly forbidden to preach to other prisoners. It was understood that whoever was caught doing this received a severe beating. A number of us decided to pay the price for the privilege of preaching, so we accepted their terms. It was a deal; we preached and they beat us. We were happy preaching. They were happy beating us, so everyone was happy."*
> --Richard Wurmbrand[19]

Richard Wurmbrand exhibited *James 1:2-5*:

"Consider it pure joy, my brothers and sisters, whenever you face trials of many kinds, because you know that the testing of your faith produces perseverance. Let perseverance finish its work so that you may be mature and complete, not lacking anything. If any of you lacks wisdom, you should ask God, who gives generously to all without finding fault, and it will be given to you."

1 Peter 2:9 says: *"For it is commendable if someone bears up under the pain of unjust suffering because they are conscious of God."*

Richard Wurmbrand was able to bear the pain of unjust suffering. He was imprisoned unjustly for his Christian faith, and he was a wonderful example to us that in our sufferings we can still live faithfully for Jesus. When I look at Richard Wurmbrand's life and the lives of other saints who have gone before me, I wonder if I would withstand suffering in the same miraculous way that they did. Would I consider it a joy to preach about Jesus to others if I knew I was going to be beaten for it?

When Suffering Comes Knocking
Do you wonder how you will react when suffering comes knocking on your door? Perhaps suffering has already come calling for you. I want to talk about what we can do in times of suffering and in times of blessing.

In Times of Suffering
When we are in a time of great trial and suffering, our biggest assignment should be to cling to God with all of our might. Peter again instructs those suffering for being a Christian: "So then, those who suffer according to God's will should commit themselves to their faithful Creator and continue to do good" (1 Peter 4:19). He goes on to say: "Humble yourselves, therefore, under God's mighty hand that he may lift you up in due time. Cast all your anxiety on him because he cares for you" (1 Peter 5:6-7).

We know that we will suffer in this world. When we do, we can cast all of our anxiety on God. He knows what we are going through and He loves to hear from us.

In Times of Blessing
Our lives will not be all intense suffering or all times of blessing. Most of us will experience both of these seasons in our lifetimes. When we are in a time of blessing, we can thank God for what He has given us. The most dangerous thing about a time of blessing is our tendency to forget God and only enjoy the blessings He has given us rather than Him. By thanking

God for the blessings we receive, we remind ourselves that God is the provider.

We can prepare for times of suffering by studying God's Word and practice gospel rhythms so that we can stay connected to the vine. Though we aren't in a time of need, we can be prepared for when that time comes. Just as Joseph prepared for the famine in Egypt by storing away grain while it was a time of blessing, we can store away God's Word in our hearts to prepare us for when we really need it.

Lastly, we can ask God to open our eyes and help us to see those in times of suffering and ask God how we can be a help to them. We can follow Paul's instruction to the Romans: *"Rejoice with those who rejoice; mourn with those who mourn" (Romans 12:15).*

We can easily forget that suffering is an effect of the fall and that we are all going to experience suffering in this world. Because we forget these facts, we are often surprised when suffering comes our way and we can blame God or be angry with Him that our circumstances are not going the way we want them to. Reminding ourselves that we will suffer in this world, but God is always with us and we are never alone can help us to face suffering with courage and strength. God has a purpose for everything that He does and His purpose in your suffering may be God drawing your heart closer to His.

HOW WE REMEMBER

What about you? Are you surprised at the fiery trials you are facing? Are you struggling in your suffering?

- If you are in the midst of a fiery trial, you can arm yourself with Truth. 2 Corinthians 1:5 says: "For just as we share abundantly in the sufferings of Christ, so also our comfort abounds through Christ." Christ is our comfort and we can lay our burdens out to Him. We can be "joyful in hope, patient in affliction, faithful in prayer" (Romans 12:12). You can also know that you are not alone: "Resist him, standing firm in the faith, because you know that the family of believers throughout the world is undergoing the same kind of sufferings" (1 Peter 5:9).

Gospel Rhythm: Living Life in the Christian Community

> *"The church is the place of the utmost importance; it is the nursery of saints, the fold of Christ, the home of His children"* - Richard Baxter

Introduction

The church has been a big part of my life for as long as I can remember. I attended Sunday school, was part of the church programs, and I was active in my youth group. As an adult, I went to other churches for a while and ended up going back to the same church I grew up in, this time around with my husband and children. For the first little bit of our marriage, I treated the church as if it was there to serve me. Later, I heard a challenge on a podcast that my church needed my participation and it changed how I viewed the church. I started signing up for Bible studies within the church and I took leadership roles when they came my way. There was a transformation in my thinking. I wanted to serve Jesus as I served the church rather than looking at ways my church could serve me. Many of us treat church similarly, looking to the church to serve us rather than giving of ourselves to the glory of God.

Now, our family is fully immersed in serving the church because my husband went to seminary in his thirties and started pastoring in a small church that we love. We have found that the more involved we are at church, the more spiritual encouragement and fellowship we receive from the church. This doesn't mean we serve the church for what we will receive; rather, it means when we give our lives away, God provides us with what we need. God established His church to provide discipleship, encouragement, guidance, and provision for His people.

The apostle Paul used marriage as an example of how Christ cared for His church:

> "Husbands, love your wives, just as Christ loved the church and gave himself up for her to make her holy, cleansing her by the washing with water through the word, and to present her to himself as a radiant church, without stain or wrinkle or any other blemish, but holy and blameless."
> Ephesians 5:25-27

Can you imagine a husband who lovingly cares for His wife as we read this passage? Jesus is lovingly caring for each of us so that we can be presented to God without blemish. No matter how bad things get here on earth, no matter how many church scandals there are, Jesus is preserving His bride. He gave Himself up for her (the church) and He is preparing her for the consummation of time when He returns. It is a wonder that we will be presented to God without stain, wrinkle, or any other blemish. What a day that will be!

> *"Then I heard what sounded like a great multitude, like the roar of rushing waters and like loud peals of thunder, shouting: 'Hallelujah! For our Lord God Almighty reigns. Let us rejoice and be glad and give him glory! For the wedding of the Lamb has come, and his bride has made herself ready. Fine linen, bright and clean, was given her to wear.'"*
> Revelation 19:6-8

Jesus is coming again and when He does, His bride will be ready. As we wait, we are to be the body of Christ here on earth. We are to build each other up with encouragement, we are to teach each other as disciples, we are to hold each other accountable, and we are to provide for each other. We all need to be active participants in the life of the body of Christ.

Encouragement

One of the main functions of the church is to encourage Christians to press on in their faith. This world can be a very inhospitable place for the children of God and we need encouragement along the way. Membership in a local church is a great way to receive encouragement as well as give encouragement to others. When the body of Christ comes together on Sundays to sing His praises and hear His Word preached, we receive the benefit of witnessing other people's faith. It is a reminder that we are not alone and this world is not all that there is. When we see other believers bearing witness to this truth, it builds us up and encourages us to continue to faithfully walk with Christ.

The Bible instructs us to encourage others:

"As iron sharpens iron, so one person sharpens another."
Proverbs 27:17

"Let us consider how we may spur one another on toward love and good deeds, not giving up meeting together, as some are in the habit of doing, but encouraging one another—and all the more as you see the Day approaching."
Hebrews 10:24-25

God expects Christians to look for opportunities to encourage others to follow Christ. Christians in the church should be iron that will sharpen others and can be sharpened by others. The church is a place where we can put this sharpening into practice.

Our ultimate goal is to be in God's presence forever in Heaven. While we wait, we want to help others inherit eternal salvation as well. When we go to church, we should be looking for ways to encourage others in the truth of God's Word. As we get ready for church and every other day for that matter, we can ask God, "Who can I help sharpen today?" We can also thank God for sending others to sharpen us as well.

God's ways are higher than our ways. Our minds trick us into thinking that we are the happiest when we receive from others rather than giving of ourselves. God's upside-down Kingdom works differently than the rest of the world. The more we encourage others around us, the more encouraged we are. We shouldn't sit back and wait for people to encourage us; we can be encouraged by pouring into others.

Discipleship
Discipleship is training each other in the way we should go. When we become disciples of Jesus, we automatically become

disciple-makers. We live with the goal of knowing Jesus and being with Him forever, as well as helping others know Jesus and be with Him forever. Part of knowing Him is being trained in how to live like Him. We want to understand Scripture, see what daily walking with Jesus means, and live lives full of joy.

The church is the primary place we can turn to be trained in the ways of Jesus. It is also the place where we use our training to train others.

> *"Then Jesus came to them and said, 'All authority in heaven and on earth has been given to me. Therefore go and make disciples of all nations, baptizing them in the name of the Father and of the Son and of the Holy Spirit, and teaching them to obey everything I have commanded you. And surely I am with you always, to the very end of the age.'"*
> Matthew 28:18-19

> *"'Come, follow me,' Jesus said, 'and I will send you out to fish for people.'"*
> Matthew 4:19

Jesus instructs us that we should make disciples of all the nations. We start by doing that in our own churches. We teach and train each other. We fish for people by passing on Jesus's teachings, especially His message of repentance for the forgiveness of sins that He commands us to teach in His name (Luke 24:47). It doesn't stop in the church. As we go about our daily lives, we will be involved with people who desperately need to hear the gospel message. We should be looking for ways that we can share the good news of Jesus with them and bring them into the church as well so that they might have fellowship with God through faith in Jesus along with us (1 John 1:3).

The church provides a way for us to observe how others meet with Jesus. The church can teach us gospel rhythms, as well as enhance our understanding and application of the Scriptures. We can also observe other people's fruit. We can see how they joyfully serve the Lord and we can strive to be an example of that for others.

> "This is to my Father's glory, that you bear much fruit, showing yourselves to be my disciples."
> John 15:8

Jesus's disciples can be recognized by knowing the truth and bearing fruit. We want to build each other up in the church to do these things. The Bible describes the imagery of sheep following their shepherd. Jesus is our Shepherd. He guides us and leads us. As we walk alongside other sheep who are following Jesus, we are also showing others what following the Shepherd looks like.

Authority

Another function of the church is to keep watch over each other. This means that we need to submit to our church's authority in our lives. If you aren't obeying Scripture, the church can lovingly point that out in your life. A church that does this well is a church that cares for the person in sin with the goal of restoration. I have heard horror stories of churches exploiting people in sin or disciplining them not as a means for restoration, but for humiliation. It is also horrible to ignore the sins of professing Christians and allow them to willfully wander from God without loving correction. The church has authority because we are often unable to see our own sins and being a member of the body of Christ helps us to identify our own sin when others lovingly call us to correction.

> *"Brothers, if someone is caught in a sin, you who are spiritual should restore him gently."*
> *Galatians 6:1*

We are called to keep watch on each other in the church, and we are also called to keep watch on ourselves. This means that when someone from the church confronts our sins, we should confess humbly and be able to be restored. When we see that someone else has committed a sin, we can do as Jesus tells us here in Matthew:

> *"If your brother or sister sins, go and point out their fault, just between the two of you. If they listen to you, you have won them over. But if they will not listen, take one or two others along, so that every matter may be established by the testimony of two or three witnesses. If they still refuse to listen, tell it to the church; and if they refuse to listen even to the church, treat them as you would a pagan or a tax collector."*
> *Matthew 18:15-17*

When we go to confront someone about their sin, we need to make sure that we are in right standing with God. This requires prayer and a close watch over our own lives as well. We need to make sure that we aren't confronting someone out of our own selfish interests, but only so they may be restored to a right relationship with God again. Notice the passage says that we should point out the fault just between the two of us first. We shouldn't make a big production and draw attention to it, but keep it between the two of us. This reveals that our goal is restoration rather than publicly embarrassing the other person.

When that person doesn't listen, then it is time to get one or two others involved. The primary goal is the restoration of the person sinning to God, and with that, we want to keep their dignity as well as we can.

> *"Why do you look at the speck of sawdust in your brother's eye and pay no attention to the plank in your own eye? How can you say to your brother, 'Let me take the speck out of your eye,' when all the time there is a plank in your own eye? You hypocrite, first take the plank out of your own eye, and then you will see clearly to remove the speck from your brother's eye."*
> Matthew 7:3-5

This passage warns us that when we confront our brother and sister, we need to make sure we don't have sin we need to take care of in our own life. After we have examined our own lives, we are better able to confront someone else about their sin. We don't ignore sin in our lives or the lives of others. We are called to confront sin in others, we just need to make sure our own lives are clear of sin first.

Church discipline is not always a cheery topic, but it is an important topic. The church that doesn't discipline is a church that isn't walking closely to Jesus. If the church is permitting sin to run free, we are tarnishing Jesus's image to nonbelievers. As Christians, we should be teachable and ready to repent, knowing that we all fall short of the glory of God. The church provides protection for us as we walk through this life. Going through life without the loving accountability of a church community is dangerous territory because we all have a tendency to justify our own sin. The church is a loving place of accountability that God has established to encourage holiness so that we can represent Jesus to the world more accurately.

Provision

The last function of the church we will discuss is provision. Churches can provide for our physical and spiritual needs. Many times, being a part of the body of Christ gives us the physical provision that we need. Meals are often brought to those who are sick or just had a baby. Churches can share what they have with the body of Christ.

> *"Carry each other's burdens, and in this way you will fulfill the law of Christ."*
> *Galatians 6:2*

> *"Now he who supplies seed to the sower and bread for food will also supply and increase your store of seed and will enlarge the harvest of your righteousness. You will be enriched in every way so that you can be generous on every occasion, and through us your generosity will result in thanksgiving to God. This service that you perform is not only supplying the needs of the Lord's people but is also overflowing in many expressions of thanks to God. Because of the service by which you have proved yourselves, others will praise God for the obedience that accompanies your confession of the gospel of Christ, and for your generosity in sharing with them and with everyone else. And in their prayers for you their hearts will go out to you, because of the surpassing grace God has given you. Thanks be to God for his indescribable gift!"*
> *2 Corinthians 9:10-15*

Life in this world is not easy, especially if you are a Christian. The local church can share the burden of their congregant's spiritual needs by praying for each other. This means the congregation needs to be vulnerable with one another so that the local congregation knows how to pray.

As members of the body of Christ, we can receive provision from the church with humility. We can share with the church our needs so that they know how to pray for us. We can give generously, knowing that Jesus will provide what we need.

Your Local Church Needs Your Involvement

You are needed in each function of the church. The church needs your voice on Sunday mornings singing praises to God. You are needed to remind others what God's Word says, the church needs you to bear others' burdens and uplift them in prayer. The church needs you to hold others accountable while still keeping watch over yourself. The church needs you to give your gifts, time, and physical provision. The church needs you to be active in the body.

Peter and I haven't always been faithful church attendees. Early in our marriage, we were members of a local congregation, but we still skipped out on a fairly regular basis. We didn't come eager to hear from God's Word or to encourage others. We weren't sharing in the body of Christ the way we should have been. Somewhere along the way, I was encouraged to be more active in my church. I joined the women's ministry Bible study and was greatly encouraged by the older women of my church. We started to make sure we were there every Sunday we could, and when we were there, we wanted to encourage others. We started using our gifts: Peter played guitar for the children's ministry and I taught Sunday School. We realized that we received far more from our church family when we fully gave ourselves to our church family.

Sometimes the needs of our local congregations will match our spiritual gifts and personal passions. However, there are other times when your local church will need you to serve in an area you are not gifted in or don't particularly enjoy. We can still serve even if we don't feel that we are gifted in that area. God will receive our humble offering and the church will benefit as we lay down our preferences for the good of the whole. When we are serving in areas that highlight our giftings we lay them down as an offering to the Lord as well knowing that our giftings came from Him. We can turn around and glorify Him with our giftings.

The Lord's Supper as a Reminder of the Gospel

Being an active member of a local church also allows us access to the Lord's Supper. When we participate in the Lord's Supper, we are reminded that Jesus gave His body and spilled His blood for our sins. It gives us a chance to search our hearts and repent of sins.

The Heidelberg Catechism says this about the Lord's Supper:

Q: How does the Lord's Supper remind you and assure you that you share in Christ's one sacrifice on the cross and in all his gifts?

A: In this way:

Christ has commanded me and all believers to eat this broken bread and to drink this cup. With this command he gave this promise: First, as surely as I see with my eyes the bread of the Lord broken for me and the cup given to me, so surely his body was offered and broken for me and his blood poured out for me on the cross.

Second, as surely as I receive from the hand of the one who serves, and taste with my mouth the bread and cup of the Lord, given me as a sure signs of Christ's body and blood, so surely he nourishes and refreshes my soul for eternal life with his crucified body and poured-out blood.[20]

The church provides us with these physical signs that remind us of the spiritual truth that Christ died for us and gives us new life through faith in Him. We are in Him and will be with Him for all eternity. This is a powerful reminder and a blessing to be able to participate in it with the body of Christ while we are here on earth.

The church body is a gift from God as we wait for Jesus's return. Participating in the body of Christ gives us encouragement, discipleship, guidance from the church's authority, and provision. Christ is preparing His bride as we wait for His return.

HOW WE REMEMBER

Do you belong to a local church congregation where you can receive encouragement, discipline, reminders, and fellowship? Are you giving yourself fully to encouraging others and giving fully to Christ's body?

It is my hope that this chapter will encourage you to invest in a church. We are meant to meet together, encourage one another, and walk together to our final home—eternal life with God.

Here are some applications for this chapter:

1. Take a look at your current status with the church. Do you belong to a church or are you trying to go it alone watching sermons online by yourself? Are you a member of a church but know you are holding back from fully giving yourself to the bride of Christ? If either of these answers are true for you, ask God to forgive you and take steps to make the correction.
2. Make sure that the church you belong to is preaching the good news from the Bible. This means you will need to know what your Bible says. You want to be fed from food that will fill you properly.

We Forget: True Joy is Only Found in God

> "There is a God-shaped vacuum in the heart of every man which cannot be filled by any created thing, but only by God, the Creator, made known through Jesus."
> - Blaise Pascal

Introduction:

This past year our family decided to get a dog. The kids had wanted one for years, but we thought they should be a little older so they could be more helpful. There was absolute pandemonium when Peter and I showed our kids the picture of the little puppy we would be bringing home the very next week.

We have had our dog for several months now, and though we all still love him and would never give him back, some of that beginning bliss has worn off. The kids don't enjoy having to take him outside or take him on walks when they are tired. The joy they thought they imagined from owning a dog isn't quite the same as the reality of owning a dog.

This disconnect is common: we get married and think that the other person will make us happy forever, we think that the new vehicle we drove off the lot will fulfill our longings, we think everything will be great when we get that new house or a new job, or that wonderful vacation. We soon find out that our spouse is a sinner who can hurt our feelings, the new vehicle depreciates as soon as it's driven off the lot, the new house is lived in and not pristine anymore, the job comes with a whole new set of frustrations, and that vacation doesn't bring permanent joy and rest. All of these examples certainly can bring temporary happiness, but they won't fill us up with lasting joy.

We often forget that our true and lasting joy can only come from God. We end up chasing after created things to feel satisfied and we find out fairly quickly that those things will not satisfy us forever, if at all. Augustine said, "You have made us for Yourself, O Lord, and our hearts are restless until they find rest in You."[23] We need to be reminded that God is the only One who brings satisfaction. Our hearts will restlessly chase after worldly things until we fill our hearts with the only One who can fully satisfy us.

Happiness vs. Joy

Happiness and joy are two emotions that get easily mixed up. Joy contrasts with happiness in that it isn't a fleeting experience. True joy is confidence in living our lives the way God wants us to, knowing that He is taking care of everything that we need. Happiness is a fleeting experience felt when we enjoy one of

WE FORGET: TRUE JOY IS ONLY FOUND IN GOD

life's pleasures that God has given us. Happiness sticks around just as long as our circumstances are favorable, but joy sticks around through hardship.

As Christians, we should ask God to help us know the difference between happiness and joy. When we start chasing temporary happiness, we need to be reminded that it won't provide lasting joy. We want our days filled with treasure that lasts. Let's look at how we can chase after lasting joy.

> *"All things are wearisome, more than one can say. The eye never has enough of seeing, nor the ear its fill of hearing."*
> Ecclesiastes 1:8

In high school and college, Peter sought after personal accomplishments and getting his name recognized. He stayed up late doing homework and pushed his body in athletics. It was a very tiring time for him. As we were talking about this later in life, he reflected, "Did I do that all for nothing?" It is hard to come to the conclusion that our accomplishments don't fill us up or even matter in the long run.

I place a high value on my personal relationships. I want my relationships to be healthy and beneficial. I end up making my husband and children idols because I place them before Jesus in my life. I start to care more about what they think than living a righteous life glorifying God. Worry is a sin in my life that stems from idolizing my relationships. I start to believe that my loved ones are in my hands, which makes me anxious for their safety. This creates a situation where my mood and outlook on life are dependent on my loved ones being okay.

I also highly value comfort, which makes me neglect important things in my life. I don't want to be pushed out of my comfort zone. The problem with never leaving my comfort zone is that growth doesn't happen quickly from hiding in comfort. I grow more when I sacrifice my personal comfort for the good of others.

We all need to critically examine what we are chasing. When we find that we are chasing temporary happiness rather than abundant joy, we can repent and ask God to forgive us, restoring us to joy.

Idolatry

Idolatry gets in the way of our pursuit of God. God's people got into trouble with idolatry when they fashioned a golden calf in Exodus 32. Moses was taking a long time to come back from meeting with God, so the Israelites made a backup plan and engaged in idol worship. The Israelites should have known they were breaking God's first two commands: 1. Don't have other gods before me and 2. You shouldn't make for yourselves an image to worship (Exodus 20).

The Interpreter's Bible dictionary defines idolatry like this: "an obsession with created things instead of devotion to the Creator."[24] The golden calf was an obsession with a created thing. The Israelites were looking to it as their help rather than to God. Don't we do the same? I have heard that a good idolatry test is to gauge your reaction if something were to be taken away. If you know the loss of an earthly treasure would make you really upset, that treasure is likely an idol in your life. No, we aren't fashioning golden calves to worship, but we worship sports and entertainment, money, sex, power, prestige, and autonomy.

The Israelites paid for their idolatry. Blood needed to be shed because it was a serious offense. Blood has been shed to pay for our idolatry as well. When we continue to chase after idols, we forget the sacrifice that Jesus paid. Chasing idols not only stomps on Jesus's beautiful gift, it also won't give us lasting joy.

Solomon's Wisdom

The author of Ecclesiastes is unknown, but some speculate that it was King Solomon, King David's son and successor. Ecclesiastes is a very candid account of his experiences with chasing after what the world has to offer and coming up empty.

> *"I, the Teacher, was king over Israel in Jerusalem. I devoted myself to study and to explore by wisdom all that is done under heaven. What a heavy burden God has laid on men! I have seen all the things that are done under the sun; all of them are meaningless, a chasing after the wind."*
> Ecclesiastes 1:12-14

Solomon teaches about the different ways that men and women search for joy in their lives: wisdom, pleasures, laughter, wine, building houses, planting vineyards, making gardens and parks, owning herds and flocks, amassing silver and gold, romantic relationships, youth, vigor, and never denying ourselves anything we want.

> *"Yet when I surveyed all that my hands had done and what I had toiled to achieve, everything was meaningless, a chasing after the wind; nothing was gained under the sun."*
> Ecclesiastes 2:11

Solomon was surveying his life. It is a good idea for all of us to do the same. We should take time to reflect and ask God if our lives are in alignment with His will for us. Solomon was receiving mercy from God. He was waking up from the fake reality that he could find joy in God's creation rather than in God Himself. He had come to realize that he would only find joy in his Creator!

> *"Whoever loves money never has money enough; whoever loves wealth is never satisfied with his income. This too is meaningless."*
> Ecclesiastes 5:10

> *"To the man who pleases him, God gives wisdom, knowledge and happiness, but to the sinner he gives the task of gathering and storing up wealth to hand it over to the one who pleases God. This too is meaningless, a chasing after the wind."*
> Ecclesiastes 2:26

This verse really gets me. It cuts straight to the futility that we often subscribe to. We work so hard to gather up wealth just to hand it off to someone else. Wealth can't save us or satisfy us. Many people will look back on their lives and realize too late that they wasted their lives, striving to gain something that is never going to satisfy them.

> *"I know that everything God does will endure forever; nothing can be added to it and nothing taken from it. God does it so that men will revere him."*
> Ecclesiastes 3:14

Solomon was getting back to our purpose again with this verse. Why are we here? We are here to glorify God. God wants us to revere Him! This is where we will find our joy!

WE FORGET: TRUE JOY IS ONLY FOUND IN GOD

"And I saw that all labor and all achievement spring from man's envy of his neighbor. This too is meaningless, a chasing after the wind."
Ecclesiastes 4:4

How many of us get caught trying to follow other people's lives? We want to keep up with those around us, so we wear ourselves out chasing meaningless activities. This, too, will leave us empty.

"Naked a man comes from his mother's womb, and as he comes, so he departs. He takes nothing from his labor that he can carry in his hand."
Ecclesiastes 5:15

Many people don't enjoy reading Ecclesiastes. It seems like a real downer. It can feel like a list of things that won't make us happy, which seems pretty depressing. I have come to really love Ecclesiastes because it paints the human condition so well. We have a loving Creator who knows that the best thing for us is to seek Him, but we chase after meaningless means in the world to bring us joy. Ecclesiastes warns that chasing these things will never bring us joy. We will find true fulfillment only in chasing after our Creator.

I have spent many years of my life chasing after "happiness" in this life, but now I am thankful that God placed His joy in my heart. I can see now that I find true joy when I am pursuing what God desires for my life rather than chasing what I desire. This doesn't mean that I never forget and get off track pursuing happiness, but it does mean that I can see the big picture. Ultimately, I know that chasing happiness will only make me happy as long as the circumstances are favorable. Lasting joy comes when I remember that I have a God who has pursued me in my sin and made a way for me to glorify Him forever. That is my life's purpose and that is what leads me to true lasting joy.

Chase the Pearl of Great Price

> *"The kingdom of heaven is like treasure hidden in a field. When a man found it, he hid it again, and then in his joy went and sold all he had and bought that field. Again, the kingdom of heaven is like a merchant looking for fine pearls. When he found one of great value, he went away and sold everything he had and bought it."*
> Matthew 13:44-46

The treasure in the field and the pearl of great price represent God. Those who are reconciled to Him through faith in Jesus recognize how valuable a treasure and pearl He is. When we recognize God as our treasure, anything else will come up short. It is good for us when they do. When we see the futility of chasing the pleasures of this world, we can better see our completeness in Jesus.

Many of us recognize the value of God's treasure, but many of us have trouble giving up everything else to attain it. We want God (our Treasure), but we also want what the world has to offer. The man who found the treasure in the field didn't hesitate. He got rid of everything he had just to attain this treasure.

I think we want God, but we can't give up our grip on the world. We don't see God as more valuable than any of these worldly treasures. This passage is not prescriptive, telling us that we should all sell everything that we own, but it does mean we should take a hard look at our lives and be ready to get rid of any idol we are clinging to. This passage exhorts us to remove anything in our lives that is holding us back from seeing God as our Treasure. It is better to lose earthly treasure than to lose our eternal life and the unsurpassing joy of knowing God.

Living with Joy

One of the themes of the Bible is a message of an upside-down Kingdom. When the world tells us that we should chase after everything that we think will make us happy, Scripture tells us to deny ourselves (Luke 9:23-24). God's Word tells us that the more we chase after what we believe will satisfy us, the more unsatisfied we will become. On the flip side, the more we deny ourselves and live for Jesus, the more satisfied we will become.

Sometimes we approach our lives like we approach eating at a buffet. We look around to see what looks pleasing to us, and then we put it on our plates. Similarly, we look around at all the options available for our life and take the initiative to change it. The problem with this way of thinking is that we have no real power to alter our lives. When we put pressure on ourselves to make our life better and more pleasing for ourselves, we fail to ask God to help us be faithful with whatever He has for us. Wendell Berry said it well: "We live the given life, and not the planned."[25] We find joy when we faithfully serve God in our days rather than striving to make our days what we desire for ourselves.

I have felt the pull of the world on my own heart, and I have felt the joy of laying my life down for others. When I get hyper-focused on serving myself, I feel drained. I feel like I am drowning and I can't keep my head above water. When I am resting in Jesus to help me provide for others, He overflows my cup. I am able to serve Him joyfully because He is providing me with everything that I need. Resting in Jesus is a key component of living a joyful life.

The Bible commands us to live with joy: "Rejoice in the Lord always. I will say it again: Rejoice!" (Philippians 4:4). Sometimes our circumstances aren't joyful, and yet the Bible tells us to rejoice always. How do we rejoice at a funeral or in other dark times of sadness? We can do this because we have a living hope!

> *"Blessed be the God and Father of our Lord Jesus Christ! According to his great mercy, he has caused us to be born again to a living hope through the resurrection of Jesus Christ from the dead, to an inheritance that is imperishable, undefiled, and unfading, kept in heaven for you, who by God's power are being guarded through faith for a salvation ready to be revealed in the last time. In this you rejoice, though now for a little while, if necessary, you have been grieved by various trials, so that the tested genuineness of your faith—more precious than gold that perishes though it is tested by fire—may be found to result in praise and glory and honor at the revelation of Jesus Christ."*
> 1 Peter 1:3-7

Jesus's death and resurrection made a way for us to be reconciled to God and inherit a living hope while we are on earth. This living hope can't be taken from us if we are in Jesus. We are warned that we will face troubles in this world, but we know that we have an eternal inheritance waiting for us. We also have the Holy Spirit's help while we wait. As we walk through various trials, we can know that God is with us. We can rejoice because our hope is in Heaven waiting for us.

WE FORGET: TRUE JOY IS ONLY FOUND IN GOD

This world is not the end for us because we will have life with Him for all eternity. Since we have a future hope in Jesus, we don't have to be swayed and tossed back and forth by the circumstances of this world. We can be joyful in everything: "Be joyful in hope, patient in affliction, faithful in prayer" (Romans 12:12).

When we look to God for our lasting joy, the ways of this world don't seem as appealing. He gives us the Holy Spirit so that we can make good choices while we wait for our eternal salvation through repentant faith in Jesus. We can live our lives right now with joy because we know that we have a future hope that can't be taken away from us.

> *"May the God of hope fill you with all joy and peace as you trust in him, so that you may overflow with hope by the power of the Holy Spirit."*
> Romans 15:13

HOW WE REMEMBER

Are you chasing the pearl of great price or things of this world? Do you find your joy and hope in God or are you trying to find it in perishable things?

1. Robert Murray M'Cheyne said, "Learn much from the Lord Jesus. For every look at yourself, take ten looks at Christ. He is altogether lovely. Such infinite majesty, and yet such meekness and grace, and all for sinners, even the chief!"[26] We look to Jesus. How can you look to Christ and receive His joy?
2. Examine the idols in your life. What are you seeking for joy that can only lead you to temporary happiness?

Gospel Rhythm: Surrender

> "True submission to God is a sweet surrender of the soul to the Lord. It is not a forced, reluctant compliance, but a joyful agreement with the will of God."
> - Jonathan Edwards

Introduction

When my daughter was a baby, I held her while listening to church in the fellowship hall because she was crying. I remember questioning God on it. I thought it would be much better for me to actually be in church worshiping with the rest of our church family, but God had a different plan for me that day. This encounter helped me to learn that my ideas are not the same as God's.

God sees the whole picture, and we see only pieces. A tapestry shows the entire picture from the front, but when you look at the back, it looks like a bunch of threads and knots everywhere. This is an example of God's view versus our view. We see the back of the tapestry, and we can't possibly understand everything that God knows from our viewpoint.

> *"As the heavens are higher than the earth, so are my ways higher than your ways and my thoughts than your thoughts."*
> *Isaiah 55:9*

I was correct that being in church is good for me, but I didn't have a spirit of surrender. I was the kid questioning their parents about their directions. God didn't want me sitting in the pews that day. He wanted me to minister to my child. I run into trouble when I start presuming what God is going to have me do each day. Instead of approaching my days with open hands, asking God where He is going to use me each day, I start calculating and making plans for myself on His behalf. I start to predetermine where God should use me. That is not what submitting to a loving God looks like.

Calculating what is best for me is a sign of a lack of trust in God. Presuming what is best for myself displays pride rather than relying on God who actually does know what is best for me. God's plans for my life aren't always going to match the plans I would have chosen for myself. I will be called to uncomfortable and sad situations because God brought me to them and they are what is best. If left to myself, I would only engage in comfortable situations that wouldn't help my faith grow. But God in His wisdom puts us where we need to be so we can grow.

Some days we are called to patiently parent well-behaved children, and other days we are called to beg God for patience as we struggle to maintain our composure with kids who are acting out. Some days we are called to gatherings with loved ones to celebrate birthdays, weddings, and anniversaries, and other days we are called to a loved one's bedside to mourn a loss. We aren't promised that every day will go well. We are promised that God will be with us.

I heard this quote that I thought sums up surrender well: "What feels like death leads to life; and what feels like life leads to death."[27] We often don't want to go down unpleasant paths, but submitting and following the directions we are given leads to life in Jesus. When we just go the easy route, our faith doesn't grow, but we will grow if we are willing to trust God's good intentions for us and follow the path that He chooses for us.

Instead of planning and calculating our own lives, we can rest in a God who holds the whole world in His hands perfectly. He cares for each of us perfectly. Jesus even modeled surrender to the Father for us perfectly. The apostle Peter describes Jesus surrendering to God in 1 Peter 2:23: "When they hurled their insults at him, he did not retaliate; when he suffered, he made no threats. Instead, he entrusted himself to him who judges justly."

Jesus suffered much and yet He entrusted Himself to God, who judges justly. If we know that God took care of Jesus and had a reason for His immense suffering, shouldn't we also entrust ourselves to Him who judges justly?

What is Surrender?

The Merriam-Webster Dictionary defines surrender as "to yield to the power, control, or possession of another upon compulsion or demand."[30] The Christian life is all about surrender. Galatians 2:20 says: "I have been crucified with Christ and I no longer live, but Christ lives in me. The life I live in the body, I live by faith in the Son of God, who loved me and gave himself for me." This means that when we are saved by Jesus, our life is no longer our own. We live to glorify and honor Christ and little by little He changes our desires to His desires.

Every part of our being exists to honor the Lord. Romans 11 tells us: "Oh, the depth of the riches of the wisdom and knowledge of God! How unsearchable his judgments and his paths beyond tracing out! Who has known the mind of the Lord? Or who has been his counselor? Who has ever given to God, that God should repay him? For from him and through him and to him are all things. To him be the glory forever! Amen! Therefore, I urge you, brothers, in view of God's mercy, to offer your bodies as living sacrifices, holy and pleasing to God—this is your spiritual act of worship" (Romans 11:33 - 12:1). Jesus is worthy of all of our praise and everything that we have. In light of that, we should offer everything that we have to honor Him. Jesus also knows the best way for us to go. When we follow Him, we are doing what is best for us, and will lead us to joyful living.

Jesus summed up how we are to follow Him by saying: "If anyone would come after me, he must deny himself and take up his cross and follow me. For whoever wants to save his life will lose it, but whoever loses his life for me and for the gospel will save it. What good is it for a man to gain the whole world, yet forfeit his soul? Or what can a man give in exchange for his soul?" (Mark 8:34b-37). When we think about living out our days submitted to God, we see that we are to deny ourselves. My first thought when I wake up in the morning is usually, "What do I want to do today?" My first thought *should* be, "What does God have for me today?" I am to deny myself and follow Him!

Jesus knows that our ultimate fulfillment will come from surrendering our lives to Him. When we lay down our wants and perceived needs to follow what Jesus has for us, we are living our true purpose. When we live our true purpose, it leads to lasting joy. As I was teaching a Bible school lesson on yielding to God's will, I asked the kids why their parents limit their sugar intake and why can't they eat ten bowls of ice cream. They all said that eating that much ice cream wouldn't be good for them. Their parents put limits and restrictions on their lives for their own good. In the same way, God doesn't want us to venture into choices and situations that will ultimately hurt us. His commandments are for our good so that we can live lives that are not only pleasing to Him, but are for our ultimate joy.

Surrendering to God is the crux of our Christian walk. When we are made alive in Christ, we die to our sin and our selfish wants and desires. This allows us to live lives that are pleasing to God. When we surrender our lives to Jesus, we don't have to live with regret. We all know what it feels like to regret a decision we have made. It is good for us to lay those poor choices down and live the way Jesus wants us to live.

Biblical Examples of Surrender

The following stories are from God's Word. They each show that God's ways are higher than our ways. Many of the directions that God gave His people in His Word don't immediately make sense, and yet, His people surrendered to His will anyway. Obeying God when it doesn't make sense is one of the best ways to surrender to Him.

Noah

In Genesis 6, God told Noah to build a huge ark for a massive flood. I can only imagine how crazy the people of that time thought Noah was. Building a huge boat is not something you can do in secret. I am guessing Noah took a lot of ridicule, and yet the end of Genesis 6:22 says, "Noah did everything just as God commanded him." Noah wasn't worried about what other people thought because he was obedient to God. Since Noah surrendered to God's will for his life, he and his whole family were saved from drowning in the worldwide flood. As Noah was undertaking this huge project, he probably wondered if he was doing the right thing. We won't always understand God's will, but we should always surrender.

Abraham

God called Abraham to leave everything he knew and start over on a new journey.

> *"The Lord had said to Abram, 'Go from your country, your people and your father's household to the land I will show you. I will make you into a great nation, and I will bless you; I will make your name great, and you will be a blessing. I will bless those who bless you, and whoever curses you I will curse; and all peoples on earth will be blessed through you.'*
> *So Abram went, as the Lord had told him;*
> *and Lot went with him."*
> *Genesis 12:1-4*

Leaving everything he knew didn't make immediate sense to Abraham. Since he submitted himself to God, Abraham is known as the father of many generations, including us who have faith in Jesus as our Savior (Romans 4:16).

Mary and Joseph

Mary was a young virgin. When the angel of the Lord told her she would conceive and be with child, Mary had to know this would bring difficulty into her life. Even though it would cause her trouble and didn't immediately make sense, Mary surrendered: *"'I am the Lord's servant,' Mary answered. 'May your word to me be fulfilled.' Then the angel left her."* Luke 1:38

> *"This is how the birth of Jesus the Messiah came about: His mother Mary was pledged to be married to Joseph, but before they came together, she was found to be pregnant through the Holy Spirit. Because Joseph her husband was faithful to the law, and yet did not want to expose her to public disgrace, he had in mind to divorce her quietly."*
> Matthew 1:18-19

Rather than quietly divorce Mary, Joseph surrendered to God's plan and followed through on the marriage. I am sure that both Mary and Joseph were terrified. The position of surrendering put Mary in a hard situation. It was not good for women in that culture not to have a man in their lives. Both Mary and Joseph's beautiful surrender brought about the birth of the Savior of the world.

The Disciples

The disciples were a group of unlikely men to be Jesus's followers. When some of them were called from their fishing nets, they dropped everything to follow Jesus. Christ's call for them to leave their nets probably didn't make much sense to them at the time. Fishing was their job, so leaving their nets put them and their families at great financial risk. Yet because of their surrender to Jesus, they were used to spread the gospel to the nations.

Later, Jesus instructed the disciples to do many things that confused them: feed a large crowd with only a small meal, stop worrying about their own glory, care for the oppressed and outcasts, and they were even sent out without extra clothing and money to proclaim the message of Jesus. They were taught to surrender their desires to glorify God with their lives. Many of the disciples thought Jesus would be a king who would take over the Roman government, but that is not the way Jesus demonstrated when He walked as a man. Jesus surrendered His life to the Father for the good of all those who love Him and have faith in Him. Jesus expects His followers to do the same.

In all of these examples, the people who surrendered their lives to God's will didn't do it perfectly, and we won't either. We all still have a tendency to sin that will plague us for the rest of our lives, but we can grow in grace and live lives in joyful surrender to Jesus. When we walk with Him throughout our days, we will have purpose and joy, and we won't have to live in regret.

Jesus

Jesus's life is a perfect example of submission to the Father. Jesus lived life in the Spirit. He prayed frequently and lived to serve His Father. Near the end of Jesus's earthly life, we get a picture of just how hard the act of surrender can be. Jesus knew that His earthly life was heading towards the cross. Jesus prayed in the garden of Gethsemane because He needed God's strength to continue. The gospel of Luke even tells us that Jesus was in anguish to the point of sweating blood (Luke 22:44). He anticipated the coming wrath of God that He would endure on behalf of sinners at the cross.

Jesus said, "Abba, Father, Everything is possible for You. Take this cup from Me. Yet not what I will, but what You will" (Mark 14:36). Jesus asked God to make another way to redeem sinners. Knowing that there was no other way, Jesus submitted Himself to God and completed the hardest test He would ever face.

Jesus surrendered to God's plan for His life in the hardest of circumstances. These hard circumstances were brought upon Jesus because God loves us. If God allowed Jesus to walk through hard things to save us, doesn't that mean God will also ask us, who are united to Jesus through faith, to surrender our own wills and walk through hard things ourselves?

How Do I Walk Daily With Jesus?

In John 15 Jesus gives a helpful picture of the vine and the branches:

> *"I am the true vine, and my Father is the gardener. He cuts off every branch in me that bears no fruit, while every branch that does bear fruit he prunes so that it will be even more fruitful. You are already clean because of the word I have spoken to you. Remain in me, as I also remain in you. No branch can bear fruit by itself; it must remain in the vine. Neither can you bear fruit unless you remain in me."*
> *John 15:1-4*

Our Christian walk means keeping our eyes on Jesus and remaining in Him. The Father, the gardener, is going to prune the branches that remain in Jesus. This means that God may allow us to walk through hard things to strengthen our faith and help us to remain in the vine. When we give up our own ideas about what is right for us, we are better able to be used for good. We remain in Jesus by knowing God's Word, praying and trusting Him to take care of us, and surrendering to His will rather than our own.

Peter and I have a wonderful marriage, but we still experience conflict. There have been many times when we have had to go to separate quarters for a bit to cool off. I have used that time in two different ways. The first way is to stew and count his record of wrongs and build a case around myself. The second way is to ask God to help me be calm, and then to ask God to show me my fault in the argument. When I ask, God has always shown me where I need to repent to Him. He has given me the strength and courage to approach Peter and apologize for my end of the argument. The times that I choose to build a case around myself drag out the argument, usually more insult and injury are piled up before we can come to reconciliation. When I surrender my need to be right, or to be apologized to first, and repent, reconciliation happens quickly. We are able to be in right relationship with each other again sooner and with less pain than taking the other route.

Daily life is filled with chances for us to surrender. There are many tasks that I don't like having to do for our family. I can ask God for the strength to surrender my will to His and serve my family rather than myself. I can surrender my need to worry about loved ones because I know that God loves them and can care for them to a much greater degree than I ever could. Forgiveness is something I can offer only in God's strength. I can surrender my checklist to Him knowing that the checklist doesn't define me – being a daughter of the King is what defines me! Anything that arises during my day can be surrendered to God.

Apart from Christ, we are ruled by our fear, pride, and control, and we want to mold and shape our lives so we don't have to be afraid. It is to our advantage to surrender to the One who knows what is best for us. Surrendering to God's will is the ultimate way to bring our purpose forward, and in turn, receive God's joy.

> **HOW WE REMEMBER**
>
> Do you try to control your circumstances? Do you presume to think you know what God wants for your life?
>
> Here are some ways we can grow our surrendering muscles:
>
> 1. We can pray on our knees with open hands in submission to God. This position helps us to know that our lives are not our own and we are to surrender to what He wants with our lives.
>
> 2. We can think of our lives as a blank canvas. Without presuming we know what is best with our time, we can ask God what He wants us to do with it. We can pray to be used by God throughout our days.
>
> 3. We can live our lives frequently thinking about what Jesus did on the cross. The lyrics from Near the Cross are helpful in thinking of day-to-day living with Jesus in our minds: *"Near the cross! O lamb of God, Bring its scenes before me; Help me walk from day to day; With its shadow o'er me."*[27]

We Forget: God Is Always With Us

> *"God's presence is not as scarce as our awareness of Him. He is present everywhere, at every moment, but our perception of His presence can be obscured by the busyness and distractions of life."* - Jerry Bridges

Introduction

I watched the most beautiful sunrise and suddenly, it disappeared behind the clouds with only a sliver of sun remaining. As the sun slipped behind the clouds, I thought, "This is the perfect illustration of the Christian walk!" Sometimes everything feels right in the world, and we feel God's presence unmistakably with us. Other times, His presence is harder to feel, just like how the sunrise is harder to see behind the clouds. The sun was still rising, even though it was harder to see. God is still with us even when we don't feel His presence.

Our lives are going to be a mix of feeling God's presence and not feeling His presence. We walk through good times and we walk through times of hardship. In both of these times, we need to remember that God is with us. When things are going well for us we have a tendency to forget that He is with us. We mistake His presence for our capabilities and we think that things must be going well because of our own efforts. When times are tough, we more readily ask for Him, because we feel a deeper need for Him, but in hard times we can also feel alone or abandoned by God. Either of these scenarios can be a danger to us if we aren't aware of God's presence with us.

I feel God's presence most profoundly when I have an urgent need. I was driving in a city about an hour away from home with all four of our kids. The tire light came on and I had no idea what I should do at that moment. I prayed and told God that He was going to have to help me because I had no idea what I would do. Thankfully, God allowed me to drive right to a place where we could get it repaired. There was a fast food restaurant nearby so the kids and I could get lunch. While we ate, they repaired our tires and all was well. It is in moments when I am begging for God's help that He shows me how involved He is in my life. I had the confidence that I wasn't alone in this situation because God led me to where I needed to be. I am so thankful that in each moment of not knowing what to do, God is still with us. When I have these moments where I feel God's presence and help in my life undoubtedly, it gives me courage to come to Him for help again and again.

We don't have to be in danger to need God's presence in our lives. Each day, there are numerous times when I have no idea what I am supposed to do. Sometimes my kids ask really hard questions or a discipline issue arises, or we all need our emotions to calm down. I am thankful that I can pray quick prayers throughout each day, "Jesus, help!" I am thankful that He is with me to help and guide me when I am in a confusing situation, to give me the right words in my relationships, and even to help me push through on something I really don't want to do. It is empowering to know that I am not alone. God is always there and I can go to Him anytime day or night. When I call on the name of the Lord, I will never get a busy signal or a voicemail box. I will get my loving Father who cares for me and wants me to rely on Him throughout my days.

The times that I remember that God is always with me are a blessing, but I also have plenty of times that I forget. I start trying to go it alone and I usually end up making a big mess. Then it dawns on me that God is there while I am in the middle of wallowing. God reminds me that He is there by prompting me to pray, having someone speak wisdom into my life, or I will even hear a song that pierces my heart. Even though I have made a mess, I am thankful for His grace that reminds me I have access to Him!

God's Promise to Us

God's Word is filled with His promises to us. I love that throughout Scripture God tells His people He will be with them: He tells Isaac (Genesis 26:3, 24), Jacob (Genesis 31:3), Moses (Exodus 3:12), Joshua (Joshua 1:9), Gideon (Judges 6:16), David (2 Samuel 7:9), Solomon (1 Kings 11:38), all of Israel (Isaiah 41:10), Jeremiah (Jeremiah 1:8), and Jesus comforts His disciples as He is about to ascend to Heaven telling them that He will be with them always to the very end of the age (Matthew 28:20).

We hear God's Word tell us in numerous places that God is with us:

> *"The Lord your God is with you,*
> *the Mighty Warrior who saves.*
> *He will take great delight in you;*
> *in his love he will no longer rebuke you,*
> *but will rejoice over you with singing."*
> *Zephaniah 3:17*

When we look at the descriptors of God in this verse we see that He is a mighty warrior who saves us. God is powerful and holds the whole world in His hands. He is the one putting breath in our lungs and yet, He still cares for us. He is with us, He takes delight in us, and He will rejoice over us with singing. It is hard to fathom that the God of the universe who created everything and is all-powerful actually cares to be with me. Not only is He with me, but He delights in me and rejoices over me with singing. What a comfort it is to be known by God.

> *"Even though I walk*
> *through the darkest valley,*
> *I will fear no evil,*
> *for you are with me;*
> *Your rod and Your staff,*
> *they comfort me."*
> *Psalm 23:4*

Psalm 23 was one of the first pieces of Scripture that I memorized, and I have recited it countless times in my life. It is comforting to know that even in my darkest valley, I don't have to fear evil because God is with me. Terrible things may happen to me, but I will never be alone. I will always have God's presence to comfort and guide me.

> "When Jesus had called the Twelve together, he gave them power and authority to drive out all demons and to cure diseases, and he sent them out to proclaim the kingdom of God and to heal the sick."
> Luke 9:1-2

I can imagine how terrified the disciples must have felt being sent out without Jesus's physical presence with them. They were able to make the journey because they had Jesus's power and authority going with them. We have the same. We don't have Jesus's physical presence here, but we do have His power and authority with us in the Holy Spirit. Whatever task God calls us to, we are equipped for it because we have God with us.

Abraham Sends His Servant to Find Isaac a Wife

Genesis 24 tells the story of Abraham asking his servant to return to his country and find a wife for his son, Isaac. Abraham's servant prayed this very specific prayer as he searched for a wife among the women of Abraham's old town, Nahor.

> "Then he prayed, 'Lord, God of my master Abraham, make me successful today, and show kindness to my master Abraham. See, I am standing beside this spring, and the daughters of the townspeople are coming out to draw water. May it be that when I say to a young woman, "Please let down your jar that I may have a drink," and she says, "Drink, and I'll water your camels too"—let her be the one You have chosen for Your servant Isaac. By this I will know that You have shown kindness to my master.'"
> Genesis 24:12-14

Shortly after the servant prayed this, Rebekah came to the well and did exactly as the servant had prayed. He knew that she was the one for Isaac because the servant asked God for clarity and God provided.

The servant told Rebekah's family about how Abraham had sent him there to find a wife for Isaac:

> *"Abraham said, 'The Lord, before whom I have walked faithfully, will send his angel with you and make your journey a success, so that you can get a wife for my son from my own clan and from my father's family. You will be released from my oath if, when you go to my clan, they refuse to give her to you—then you will be released from my oath.'"*
> Genesis 24:40-41

The servant could be confident on this mission because he knew he wasn't going alone. He had God's angel with him, and he knew the journey would be a success. He prayed a specific prayer, expecting God to show him exactly the right woman. God was with the servant, and He is with us as well.

We can have this confidence in our lives. We can ask God to help us with anything we need as long as it lines up with His will for us.

God's Plan for Creation

When you look at the Word of God as a whole, there are themes woven throughout. One of these themes is that God intends to dwell among His people. God began by walking with Adam and Eve in the garden, then dwelt among the Israelites with the tabernacle, and then the temple in Jerusalem. God dwelt with us in human form in the person of Jesus, and He currently dwells in all true Christians through the Holy Spirit. Ultimately, God intends to dwell with us in Heaven, where there will be no more pain and suffering and we will be in His presence forever.

Garden

God created the heavens and the earth, plants, and animals, and then the first humans. God walked in the garden with Adam and Eve (Genesis 3:8). God intended to live with His creation, but then Adam and Eve sinned and were no longer able to be with God in the garden.

Tabernacle

God instructed Moses and the rest of His people to build a tabernacle so that He could dwell among His people.

> *"Let them make me a sanctuary, that I may dwell in their midst."*
> *Exodus 25:8*

> *"I will dwell among the people of Israel and will be their God. And they shall know that I am the Lord their God, who brought them out of the land of Egypt that I might dwell among them. I am the Lord their God."*
> *Exodus 29:45-46*

The tabernacle was a tent made of fabric that held the Ark of the Covenant, where God's presence dwelt among His people. Moses was able to meet with God in this holy place (Exodus 33). After the tabernacle was built, the glory of the Lord filled it (Exodus 40). God's glory filling the tabernacle showed that God's presence was there with His people.

Temple
Solomon built the temple and blessed it and it was filled with the Lord's presence (1 Kings 8:10-11 & 27).

Jesus
Jesus walking on earth was truly God's presence dwelling with us. Jesus's life allowed us to experience God in the physical world. The life of Jesus on earth demonstrated how God loves us, pursues us, and made a way for sinners like us to dwell with God forever. Hebrews 1:3 says: "The Son is the radiance of God's glory and the exact representation of his being, sustaining all things by his powerful word. After he had provided purification for sins, he sat down at the right hand of the Majesty in heaven."

Jesus was called Emmanuel, which means "God with us." In the Incarnation, Jesus dwelt among us and revealed the glory of God in human form. John 1:14 says: "The Word became flesh and made his dwelling among us. We have seen his glory, the glory of the one and only Son, who came from the Father, full of grace and truth." When John says, "He made his dwelling among us," it means He tabernacled among us. He condescended to us for our good. It didn't benefit Jesus to leave Heaven, but He chose to come and dwell among sinful humans as a human so He could pay the ransom for our sin and allow us a way back to dwell in the presence of God the Father.

Let's rewind back to the Temple and Tabernacle for just a second. The Temple was arranged in a similar way to the Tabernacle. There was a Holy Place and a Most Holy Place where the Ark of the Covenant was located. In both the Tabernacle and Temple, there was a curtain separating the Holy Place from the

Most Holy Place. No one was allowed to enter the Most Holy Place except the high priest on the Day of Atonement. The high priest could enter the Most Holy Place, but never without blood and only once per year (Hebrews 9:7).

When Jesus died, the curtain in the Temple separating the Holy Place from the Most Holy Place was torn in two (Matthew 27:51). This signified that God's presence would be accessible to His people. The sacrifice of Jesus for our sins on the cross removed the barrier from God to us and we are able to be accepted into the Father's presence on the basis of Christ's righteousness that is imputed to all who look to Him with repentant faith. The old sacrificial system was taken away and we have direct access to God.

Holy Spirit

When Jesus ascended to Heaven, He told His disciples about the gift of the Holy Spirit. Now, those who trust in Jesus for the forgiveness of their sins receive the Holy Spirit. We have God's presence with us wherever we go.

Since the presence of God constantly dwells within believers, let's discuss ten functions of the Holy Spirit so that we can see how God's presence dwelling within us impacts our lives. The Holy Spirit has many functions:

1. The Holy Spirit gives us the words we need to say. Jesus taught that the Holy Spirit is a gift we all need: "Whenever you are arrested and brought to trial, do not worry beforehand about what to say. Just say whatever is given you at the time, for it is not you speaking, but the Holy Spirit" (Mark 13:11). We don't have to

know the right things to say – we can rely on the Holy Spirit to help us.

2. The Holy Spirit reveals to us God's plans. When Jesus was born, God revealed to Simeon that he would get to meet the promised Messiah: "It had been revealed to him by the Holy Spirit that he would not die before he had seen the Lord's Messiah" (Luke 2:26). We can count on the Holy Spirit to reveal what we need. He reveals God's plans to us in the Scriptures that He inspired. Now He helps us understand those Scriptures so that we can know God's plan for us.

3. The Holy Spirit guides and leads us. Jesus was guided by the Holy Spirit in Luke 4:1-2: "Jesus, full of the Holy Spirit, left the Jordan and was led by the Spirit into the wilderness, where for forty days he was tempted by the devil. He ate nothing during those days, and at the end of them he was hungry." Going to the wilderness for forty days doesn't sound like fun. The Holy Spirit guided Jesus where He needed to go and the Holy Spirit will guide us also. We need the Holy Spirit to guide us especially into places we don't want to go because we won't naturally go there ourselves. He also guides us into obedience and proper attitudes of the heart like worship, repentance, and faith.

4. The Holy Spirit teaches us and reminds us who God is. Jesus told His disciples in John 14:26: "But the Advocate, the Holy Spirit, whom the Father will send in my name, will teach you all things and will remind you of everything I have said to you." Although the disciples were not going to have Jesus's presence on earth

anymore, they would have the Holy Spirit who would teach them and remind them of Jesus's teaching. We didn't get to see Jesus as He walked on earth, but we all receive His teaching and are reminded of Him through the Holy Spirit, who reveals to us what Jesus said in the Word of God.

5. The Holy Spirit gives us power and helps us to be bold. Jesus tells His disciples in Acts 1:8: "But you will receive power when the Holy Spirit comes on you; and you will be my witnesses in Jerusalem, and in all Judea and Samaria, and to the ends of the earth." The Christian life is not for the faint of heart. We will be challenged and asked to move out of our comfort zones for God's glory. The Holy Spirit will give us the boldness and power that we need in these moments.

6. The Holy Spirit gives us encouragement and joy. Right after Paul converted to Christianity, the church enjoyed a break from persecution. Acts 9:31 says, "Then the church throughout Judea, Galilee and Samaria enjoyed a time of peace and was strengthened. Living in the fear of the Lord and encouraged by the Holy Spirit, it increased in numbers." The Holy Spirit gives us encouragement and joy as we live out our days glorifying God.

7. The Holy Spirit warns us, convicts us of sin, washes us, and renews us. We are blind to our own sin and we need the conviction of the Holy Spirit so we can repent. Paul wrote to Titus: "At one time we too were foolish, disobedient, deceived and enslaved by all kinds of passions and pleasures. We lived in malice and envy, being hated and hating one another. But when the kindness

and love of God our Savior appeared, He saved us, not because of righteous things we had done, but because of his mercy. He saved us through the washing of rebirth and renewal by the Holy Spirit, whom he poured out on us generously through Jesus Christ our Savior, so that, having been justified by his grace, we might become heirs having the hope of eternal life" (Titus 3:3-7). We also need the Holy Spirit to warn us of dangers and threats from others. Paul said in Acts 20:23: "I only know that in every city the Holy Spirit warns me that prison and hardships are facing me." We can trust the Holy Spirit's warnings both for our own sin and what may lie ahead for us.

8. The Holy Spirit sanctifies us. Paul writes in Romans 15:15-16: "Yet I have written you quite boldly on some points to remind you of them again, because of the grace God gave me to be a minister of Christ Jesus to the Gentiles. He gave me the priestly duty of proclaiming the gospel of God, so that the Gentiles might become an offering acceptable to God, sanctified by the Holy Spirit." Just like the Gentiles that Paul said were being sanctified by the Holy Spirit, we also are sanctified by Him. We can't be holy on our own. We need the Holy Spirit's help to make us more and more like Jesus.

9. The Holy Spirit makes our bodies temples and gives us fellowship with God. Paul writes to the Corinthians: "Do you not know that your bodies are temples of the Holy Spirit, who is in you, whom you have received from God? You are not your own; you were bought at a price. Therefore honor God with your bodies" (1

Corinthians 6:19-20). As Christians, our bodies are the temple of the Holy Spirit. We have Him with us everywhere because He dwells in us. The Holy Spirit also gives us fellowship. "May the grace of the Lord Jesus Christ, and the love of God, and the fellowship of the Holy Spirit be with you all" (2 Corinthians 13:14). Since we have the Holy presence of God dwelling in us, we are truly not alone.

10. Lastly, The Holy Spirit gives us the assurance of salvation. When we feel the Holy Spirit's presence in our lives, we can rest assured that we are born again into Christ's righteousness and we have the promise of eternal life with God. Paul tells the Ephesians: "And you also were included in Christ when you heard the message of truth, the gospel of your salvation. When you believed, you were marked in him with a seal, the promised Holy Spirit, who is a deposit guaranteeing our inheritance until the redemption of those who are God's possession—to the praise of his glory" (Ephesians 1:13-14).

Heaven
We will one day dwell in the presence of God forever. Heaven is the consummation of God's plan to be with His people. These verses from Revelation make me so excited to see this day come to fruition: "And I heard a loud voice from the throne saying, "Look! God's dwelling place is now among the people, and he will dwell with them. They will be his people, and God himself will be with them and be their God. He will wipe every tear from their eyes. There will be no more death or mourning or crying or pain, for the old order of things has passed away"

(Revelation 22:3-4). What a glorious day it will be when we are in the presence of God forever.

We can easily forget that God is always with us. It is easy to live our days only thinking about our to-do lists, but God reminds us that He is with us. He will help us and never leave us. We have access to Him through Jesus's sacrifice of atonement, which is applied to us by the Holy Spirit through faith. No matter what we face, we aren't doing it alone. We can glorify God with confidence knowing that the same power that raised Jesus from the grave lives in us (Ephesians 1:19-21).

> *"For I am convinced that neither death nor life, neither angels nor demons, neither the present nor the future, nor any powers, neither height nor depth, nor anything else in all creation, will be able to separate us from the love of God that is in Christ Jesus our Lord."*
> Romans 8:38-39

HOW WE REMEMBER

Do you have a hard time remembering that God is with us and takes care of us through our days? Do you have a hard time feeling His presence?

Here are some things you can do:

1. Practice being in God's presence, like Mary sitting at Jesus's feet (Luke 10:39). Worship Him, ask Him throughout your days what He wants you to do, and come back and tell Him thank you for those answered prayers when all we have is a quick plea, "Jesus, help!"
2. Before we engage the world, we should enjoy being in His presence. When we get our cups filled by God in the mornings, we will more readily recognize His presence with us throughout our days.

Gospel Rhythm: Praise

> "A good hymn not only stirs the emotions but also engages the mind. It should be filled with sound theology that reinforces our understanding of God and His Word."
> -Keith Getty

Introduction

There have been times in my life when I have felt like I was doing exactly what God created me to do. When I am helping my children with their school work or discussing a catechism or Bible verse, I feel that I am doing exactly what I was created to do. The movie *Chariots of Fire* depicts the life of Eric Liddell, the Olympian who dropped out of his race because it was going to be held on a Sunday. Eric was to represent England and he was favored to win, but he wouldn't participate because of his convictions. The movie quotes Eric as saying, "When I run, I feel God's pleasure." I think we could all insert this phrase into anything we are doing that is praising God with our whole hearts. When I praise God, I feel God's pleasure.[28]

Praising God is what we were created for. There are many ways to praise God with our lives: through giving thanks, music, art, obeying Him, and any activity that glorifies God and we feel His pleasure. This chapter will focus on giving thanks and music.

Our family incorporates a family worship time into our week. This is a time for us to praise God together. It usually consists of a time for reflecting on how God revealed Himself to us each week by writing down what we are thankful for. We share what we were thankful for with each other and then we move on to singing our hymn of the month.[31] Our family takes turns picking a hymn to sing every day (or every day we can) that month. Through this process, we save the hymns in a binder and then we can look back and pick from hymns we have used in the past. We don't read from Scripture at family worship time because we incorporate reading Scripture into our meal times (but adding Scripture to family worship time is an excellent idea). We wrap up our worship with prayer and everyone takes turns praying through the P.R.A.Y. method that was outlined earlier.

Praising God as a family doesn't always look as we think it should. Sometimes, we come with grumbling attitudes and hearts that aren't ready to worship. I don't want you to think that our family praises God perfectly, but we do intentionally come together to praise God. We want worship to be a primary function of our lives.

Thanksgiving

Though Thanksgiving is not a traditional Christian holiday, the practice of giving thanks draws us nearer to the heart of God. Thanksgiving is one of my favorite holidays because it's encouraging to not only give thanks, but also to hear what other people are thankful for. When we direct our thanksgiving to God, we recognize that all good things come from Him. This cuts through our pride and our anxiety because we are acknowledging everything comes from God and we owe our gratitude to Him.

A big part of giving thanks is stopping to notice the things around you. Our lives are very busy and we are always thinking ahead to what needs to be done next. Many of us have a hard time stopping to notice all the gifts that surround us. I was convicted of my tendency to rush to the next thing when I was teaching a Sunday School class. Part of the lesson was to stand outside and just take some breaths and notice what was going on. As we stood outside I could hear the birds singing, which is something I had rarely noticed before. When we slow down to notice all of creation around us, we can thank God for providing what we need and giving us even more than what we need.

Command to Give Thanks

After the Ark of the Covenant was brought to Jerusalem, King David gave thanks to God. David's praise to God is recorded in 1 Chronicles 16:

> "Give thanks to the Lord, call on his name; make known among the nations what he has done. Sing to him, Sing praise to him; tell of all his wonderful acts. Glory in his holy name; let the

hearts of those who seek the Lord rejoice. Look to the Lord and his strength; seek his face always. Remember the wonders he has done, his miracles, and the judgments he pronounced."
1 Chronicles 16:8-12

David gives a picture of praise to his people: give thanks to the Lord, call on His name, make Him known among the nations, sing praise, tell of His wonderful acts, glory in His holy name, rejoice, look to the Lord, seek His face, and remember the wonders He has done. We glorify God when we participate in any of these practices. It pleases God when we turn to Him with all of our hearts.

David certainly had negative qualities, but he was a man after God's own heart because he was not only quick to repent but also kept his eyes on God. He made it his whole life's mission to praise God, and I am thankful for the Psalms that he left behind, which give us a great example of glorifying God. May we follow in David's footsteps and give God praise and glory like David did.

Music

Music has a way of planting itself inside a person. Recently I started singing a nonsense jingle and Peter finished it for me. We both tried to recall where it came from and neither of us could figure it out. This experience exemplifies that music finds a way to stick with us longer than words alone.

Music has many benefits, not only for our moods and emotions, but also in helping us memorize Scripture. It has been used throughout Christian history to tell the wonderful story of Jesus and His love. I love thinking about generation after generation of families singing together to remember Jesus Christ and His gift to us on the cross.

One morning recently I woke up and started scurrying about trying to get ready for my day rather than spending time in prayer focusing on God. It hit me that I had all these fearful and anxious thoughts running through my mind and I started to sing, *"I will cast all my cares upon You, I'll lay all of my burdens down at Your feet, and anytime I don't know what to do, I will cast all my cares upon You."*[32] Just singing those words cut through the fear and anxiety and served as the prayer I had desperately needed but had skipped that morning. God-honoring music can calm our anxieties and remind us that God is with us in all we do.

Music can also bind us together in worship to God. It is such a blessing to get to sing praise to God in fellowship with other believers also worshiping. I don't know how many times I have teared up hearing our sweet kids singing spiritual truths to God in worship. It is one of my greatest blessings as a parent to get to hear these lovely voices glorify God. I also love hearing the body of Christ in church glorify His name. We are especially blessed that in our small congregation we have so many voices that sing out and encourage us in worship.

Music is a special gift from God to help embolden us here on earth. It has seen people through many hard times. When the slaves were in the cotton fields in early American history, they sang spirituals to get them through their hard days. Singing is portable. The slaves were able to take these songs that contained powerful truths with them while they worked and it served to remind them that God was with them. They weren't able to pull out their Bibles for reminders, but they were able to encourage and comfort each other with the music they sang throughout their days.

We need to monitor the kind of music we allow to influence us. I recalled earlier that Peter and I had memorized a jingle without any recollection of where it came from. We need to be careful that we are putting God's truth inside us rather than harmful cultural messages. Cultural messages will always be there. When it comes time to listen to music, we want to make sure we are inserting truth into our lives.

Command to Sing
The Bible gives plenty of commands to sing praises to God. It is the second most common command in Scripture:

> *"My lips will shout for joy when I sing praise to you—*
> *I whom you have delivered."*
> *Psalm 71:23*

We can praise God for the things He has done for us. One of the main themes of Christian music is how God has delivered us from our sins.

> *"It is good to praise the Lord and make music to your name,*
> *O Most High,*
> *proclaiming your love in the morning*
> *and your faithfulness at night,*
> *to the music of the ten-stringed lyre and the*
> *melody of the harp."*
> *Psalm 92:1-3*

> *"Praise the Lord, for the Lord is good;*
> *sing praise to his name, for that is pleasant."*
> Psalm 135:3

Again we see the psalmist praising God for His attributes. Singing is a lovely way to remember all God's attributes and encourage others to remember them.

> *"Come, let us sing for joy to the Lord;*
> *let us shout aloud to the Rock of our salvation."*
> Psalm 95:1

> *"Shout for joy to the Lord, all the earth,*
> *burst into jubilant song with music;*
> *make music to the Lord with the harp,*
> *with the harp and the sound of singing,*
> *with trumpets and the blast of the ram's horn—*
> *shout for joy before the Lord, the King."*
> Psalm 98:4-6

We won't always have God's Word available to us, and we won't always be in the church setting, but when we sing songs that tell us about God and praise Him for His works, we can praise Him anywhere we go! Music gives expression to our thankfulness. God is glorified when we sing songs of praise to Him.

> *"Do not get drunk on wine, which leads to debauchery. Instead,*
> *be filled with the Spirit, speaking to one another with psalms,*
> *hymns, and songs from the Spirit. Sing and make music from*
> *your heart to the Lord, always giving thanks to God the Father*
> *for everything, in the name of our Lord Jesus Christ."*
> Ephesians 5:18-20

Not only are we commanded to praise God, but we are also commanded to "Let the message of Christ dwell among you richly as you teach and admonish one another with all wisdom through psalms, hymns, and songs from the Spirit, singing to God with gratitude in your hearts" (Colossians 3:16).

This means that we guard what goes in our ears. We should have an arsenal of songs that tell us the message of the whole Bible. Knowing all of God's character and not just His love for us helps us to have a complete picture and see the depth of who He is. We don't just worship God in some of His characteristics, but all of them. We should make sure that the songs we are singing are the full story of who Jesus is.

The songs we sing should remind us of the true God. Our finite minds like to soften God or make Him like us. God is like no other and we need to sing songs of worship that worship who He truly is. C.S. Lewis described Aslan, the character representing God in his book *The Lion, The Witch, and The Wardrobe* like this: "'Safe?' said Mr. Beaver. 'Who said anything about safe? 'Course he isn't safe. But he's good. He's the King, I tell you.'" Another character describes Aslan this way: "He's wild, you know. Not a tame lion."[33]

God is not what we want Him to be. God is who He is. He is compassionate, faithful, generous, good, holy, loving, merciful, patient, and righteous; but He is also incomprehensible, jealous, just, sovereign, and wrathful. God embodies all the good that we could ever understand. He loves us and is patient with us. God also hates unrighteousness. He wants justice to be done and He will be the one who executes justice in the world. We can't put God in a box. We need to worship Him for who

He is, not what we want Him to be. We need to make sure that the music we sing worships the One True God, not a god we made up in our minds.

Hymn Writers and Their Hymns

I find the lives of old hymn writers so intriguing. It is interesting to hear the life circumstances behind some of my favorite hymns. This next section will explore hymn writers' lives and what was going on behind the scenes of their hymns. Hearing the stories behind these rich lyrics gives me courage, makes me feel God's love for me, and makes me feel like I am in good company. Sometimes the Christian life is lonely because we live counter-culturally. Hearing rich and meaningful lyrics and also hearing the life story that accompanies them encourages me to keep going on my Christian walk.

Louisa M.R. Stead

Louisa wrote the hymn *"'Tis So Sweet to Trust in Jesus"* after her husband drowned trying to save a boy from drowning in the ocean. She was left as a single mother with a four-year-old daughter. In her grief, she wrote this song.

> *"I'm so glad I learned to trust Thee,*
> *Precious Jesus, Savior, Friend;*
> *And I know that Thou art with me,*
> *Wilt be with me to the end."*

Knowing that Louisa wrote this song after her husband drowned is a comfort because she still trusted that God would be with her to the end. Even though life had been hard, she knew God was still with her.[34]

Fanny Crosby

Due to improper medical treatment, Fanny Crosby was blind. Even though she was struck with this ailment, she wrote 8,000 hymns and she never allowed herself to become bitter. She wrote one of my favorite hymns, *"Blessed Assurance."*

> *"Blessed assurance, Jesus is mine!"*
> *Oh, what a foretaste of glory divine!*
> *Heir of salvation, purchase of God,*
> *Born of His Spirit, washed in His blood!"*

Being born of the Spirit here on earth we can look forward to glory divine in heaven! It is so wonderful to have assurance in Jesus.[32]

Horatio Spafford

Horatio was a man who was no stranger to suffering. He lost his only son to scarlet fever and only three years later lost four daughters as they were crossing the ocean. As Horatio went across the sea in a separate boat to meet his wife who was the lone survivor, he wrote the hymn, *"It Is Well With My Soul."* Though in deep anguish, Horatio wrote beautiful words about God being with us in everything.

> *"When peace like a river attendeth my way,*
> *When sorrows like sea billows roll;*
> *Whatever my lot, thou has taught me to say,*
> *It is well, it is well with my soul."*

He tells us that no matter what we are going through, we can trust God to care for us. It can be well with our souls. Throughout our human lives we are going to experience the whole range of emotions and our souls can be well in all of it.[32]

John Newton

John Newton was a troubled young man who grew up participating in the slave trade. After he was converted to Christianity, he became a minister and found hymns lacking for his congregation. He set out to write some hymns, and that is how we have "*Amazing Grace.*"

> "*Amazing grace! How sweet the sound*
> *That saved a wretch like me!*
> *I once was lost, but now am found;*
> *Was blind, but now I see.*"

Amazing Grace highlights our need for Jesus. We all know that we owe a debt that we can't pay. Though our backgrounds may not be as complicated as John Newton's, we all fall short of the glory of God. What a gift His grace is![32]

There are more ways to praise God than to give Him thanks and to sing songs of praise to God, but these two ways of praising God can bring such joy and peace to our hearts. God made us to glorify Him and when we do that in any form, we are truly doing what we were made to do. Praising God is a gift to us because we receive joy and satisfaction when we praise God. There are times when I feel far from God, and sometimes I will find a way to praise God in thanksgiving or singing songs of praise to Him. Often, when I look for a way to praise God and praise Him, I find that I don't feel distant from Him anymore. He is worthy of all of our praise, let's spend our days doing just that.

HOW WE REMEMBER

Are you able to fill up on God-honoring music? Are you soaking in the world's ideas of what is right? Here are some ways we can incorporate music into our lives.

1. Our family does a family hymn sing. We got this idea from one of the Sing Conferences that Keith and Kristyn Getty hold each year. Each month, we pick a hymn, discuss it as a family, and sing it every day (or as many days as we can). This has been such a growing experience for us, and I love singing with our family.
2. Music is very portable. We can take it with us in the car, we can listen while we are doing chores, and we can take it with us as we exercise. No matter what you do in your day, you probably have a way of incorporating music into it. I love listening to hymns while I prepare supper for the family.
3. Music also helps us to memorize Scripture. Our favorite places to find Scripture put to music are in the Seeds Family Worship albums, Psalms by Caroline Cobb, and Andrew Peterson also wrote a few songs that are based on Scripture. It is such a neat way to help get Scripture into your head and your heart.

We Forget: Our Time is Limited

"There is no evil so great that God cannot bring joy and goodness from it. That is why death deserves our attention in life. Because we instinctively want to avoid it, to turn our face away, it is good to look death in the eye and constantly remind ourselves that our hope is in God, who defeated death." -Rob Moll

Introduction

Disney Parks had a brilliant ad campaign about ten years ago. The catchphrase was: "Jaime at 14 and you. Available for a limited time only."[35] This really tugs at my parental heartstrings. As a parent, I see these moments slipping through my fingers. As I watch old videos of the kids, I really understand that each age is truly only available for a "limited time only." Raising kids has a way of speeding time up. When I was a kid, I felt like my time was unlimited! But the older I get, the more I see that my time certainly has a limit. With this thought comes intentionality. I want my life to matter. I want my days to be useful and I want God to say, "Well done, good and faithful servant" (Matthew 25:23).

I am reminded of my frailty often. I have had a few close calls that remind me that I don't have forever in this world. When Peter and I were dating, I was driving back from visiting him one weekend and I spun my car across two divided highways because I was reaching for a CD. I still can't believe that I didn't have even a scratch! A police officer and a nice man were able to help me drive right out of the ditch, and I drove home like nothing happened. There have been a few times when our kids have choked, or we couldn't find one of them, and these moments can induce similar panic. We cried out for God to help us and He did each time. When these things happen, it pulls me out of my regular routine and ways of thinking, reminding me that nothing I have is permanent. My only guarantee in this life is that Jesus is my Savior.

It is good for me to think about my days being limited. It is good for me to rehearse how I want to age and even how I want to die. Our culture hates death and aging. We avoid signs of aging by doing all we can to make it look like we aren't aging. We avoid death. We don't want to talk about it, think about it, or be near it. Avoiding the topic of aging and death doesn't delay them or make them go away. Aging and death are coming for all of us. Our bodies are aging and marching towards death every second of every day.

I understand that thinking about death is not pleasant. Death is a natural part of life. We all know that we have an expiration date. We know that our time is limited. It is good for us to think about how God would have us use that time. It is good for us to be prepared for our deaths and the deaths of those we love.

In the book *Pilgrim's Progress*, Christian ends up in a town called Vanity Fair as he journeys to the Celestial City. Vanity Fair had everything you could dream of to enjoy there. The town ended up distracting pilgrims from making progress on their journey. Many people would never leave Vanity Fair to go to the Celestial City. When Christian and his companion, Hopeful, tried to warn the people of the town about getting stuck there, the townspeople got very angry and didn't want to hear it. I see the same with us today. We don't want to hear the warnings. We don't want to think about death. We just want to enjoy ourselves as long as we can.

We Are Under the Curse of Death
We live in this world under the curse of death. Each of us is headed for an eternal future. We will spend eternity with God's presence in Heaven or without God's presence in hell. Because of the curse of sin, our presence on earth is only temporary. I often try to create heaven here on earth, and it just doesn't work. My body is going to age and wear out. I am going to be separated from loved ones by death. This earth is not all that there is. In fact, this life I am living right now is but a breath compared to eternity. Even if I live to be one hundred, one hundred years compared to eternity is nothing!

How We Cope with Mortality
We know that death is coming for us all and we will face one of two eternities. For many of us, thinking about our mortality is a

hard reality. We don't want to have to feel the curse of death, so we cope by ignoring it. We keep death at arm's length and we try to distract ourselves from thinking about it. We want to forget that our time and our loved ones' time is limited.

Jesus gives many warnings against this in God's Word. Luke 16 teaches a parable about a rich man and a poor man named Lazarus. While they were both living on earth, the rich man enjoyed many pleasures and Lazarus was starving and homeless. When they each came to die, the rich man went to hell and Lazarus went to Heaven. The rich man could see Lazarus in Heaven with Father Abraham and said: "Father Abraham, have pity on me and send Lazarus to dip the tip of his finger in water and cool my tongue, because I am in agony in this fire." But Abraham replied, "Son, remember that in your lifetime you received your good things, while Lazarus received bad things, but now he is comforted here and you are in agony" (Luke 16:24-25). The rich man then begged them to warn his brothers about the agony he was in.

This parable of Jesus warns of treating this life as if it is Heaven. We aren't promised everything that we want here on earth. Our reward is waiting for us in eternity. When we try to make this earth Heaven, we lose sight of our ultimate goal and we distract ourselves from remembering what is most important. The rich man enjoyed a comfortable life while living on earth. He distracted himself from being ready for his eternal future. He only realized his mistake when he entered eternity. At that point he knew being ready for eternity was more important than his day-to-day activities on earth. He begged them to warn his brothers from entering the same fate. By that point, it was too late. We need to do the work of preparing for eternity while we are on earth.

We can get so immersed in the world around us that we push any thoughts of death away and live our lives without thinking about it very often. Then tragedy strikes, we remember for a brief time that death is coming for us all. Then the memory starts to fade and we go back to not thinking about death.

Heed two more warnings from Jesus:

Warning #1:

> *"Therefore keep watch, because you do not know on what day your Lord will come. But understand this: If the owner of the house had known at what time of night the thief was coming, he would have kept watch and would not have let his house be broken into. So you also must be ready, because the Son of Man will come at an hour when you do not expect him."*
> *Matthew 24:42-44*

These verses focus solely on Jesus's return, but they can apply to our own deaths as well. At any time, our lives could end by death or by Jesus returning. We need to be ready for either of these outcomes. We need to remind ourselves of gospel truths and live in a manner that is pleasing to the Lord. We can also spend our time encouraging others and preparing others for their eventual deaths.

Warning #2:

> *"And he told them this parable: 'The ground of a certain rich man yielded an abundant harvest. He thought to himself, "What shall I do? I have no place to store my crops."*

Then he said, "This is what I'll do. I will tear down my barns and build bigger ones, and there I will store my surplus grain. And I'll say to myself, 'You have plenty of grain laid up for many years. Take life easy; eat, drink and be merry.'"

But God said to him, "You fool! This very night your life will be demanded from you. Then who will get what you have prepared for yourself?" This is how it will be with whoever stores up things for themselves but is not rich toward God.'"
Luke 12:16-21

The rich man in this parable was looking at earthly things. He wanted a place to store his crops. I also think about earthly things before godly things. It is hard not to be focused on what is right in front of us because that is what we see. Heavenly things seem so far away and the urgency doesn't feel as strong as the ways of life right before our eyes. We want good things while we are living in this world, but God reminds the rich man and us that our lives could end at any moment. We are not promised tomorrow and we should work to store up treasures in Heaven rather than on earth.

Everything we own in this world will one day not be ours. "By the sweat of your brow you will eat your food until you return to the ground, since from it you were taken; for dust you are and to dust you will return" (Genesis 3:19). Our lives shouldn't be spent trying to get rich and preserve our comfort and strength here on earth. Our lives should be spent storing up treasures in Heaven. "Do not store up for yourselves treasures on earth, where moths and vermin destroy, and where thieves break in and steal. But store up for yourselves treasures in heaven, where moths and vermin do not destroy, and where thieves do not break in and steal" (Matthew 6:19-20).

Storing treasures in Heaven means living lives in obedience to God here on earth. We should tell others about God and yearn for them to receive eternal salvation with us. When we disciple others, we are storing up treasures in Heaven.

Jesus Defeated Death

Now for the good news! Jesus has defeated death with His life, death, and resurrection. The author of Hebrews tells us: "Since the children have flesh and blood, he too shared in their humanity so that by his death he might break the power of him who holds the power of death—that is, the devil—and free those who all their lives were held in slavery by their fear of death" (Hebrews 2:14-15). Jesus has defeated death, so we don't need to fear it.

We Can Live Lives Unafraid of the Curse of Death

Athanasius said, "But now that the Savior has raised His body, death is no longer terrible, but all those who believe in Christ tread it underfoot as nothing, and prefer to die rather than deny their faith in Christ, knowing full well that when they die they do not perish, but live indeed, and become incorruptible through the resurrection."[36]

I have heard different accounts of people dying and it goes one of two ways. The person dying has a peace surrounding them, or they didn't have peace, experiencing pure terror in their final moments. When we trust Jesus for the forgiveness of our sins, we can face death with peace. We can tread death underfoot as though it is nothing because we know that our eternal future is secure.

I have learned a few things watching my loved ones die. I admire my loved ones who made an effort to help their family after they were gone. It takes maturity to make sure those left behind are taken care of, not only physically but spiritually and emotionally, too. Rather than spend their time struggling against death, they were preparing for it and trusting God in their final days.

I haven't met the following two people, but their deaths inspire me to walk toward my death with the same grace and eagerness, knowing that our reward is in Heaven!

Tim Keller

Tim Keller was a prominent American pastor who died in the spring of 2023 from cancer. While he was dying, his words to his son were: "There is no downside for me leaving, not in the slightest." Tim Keller knew he was to receive his crown in glory. He modeled dependence on God as he walked toward his death.[37]

Joey Feek

Joey Feek was a country music singer in the band Joey + Rory. She died of cancer at forty years old. As she was battling cancer she told people, "I win either way. If I go to Heaven, I win and if I stay here on earth, I win."[38]

This models after Paul's admission to the church in Philippi:

> "For to me, to live is Christ and to die is gain. If I am to go on living in the body, this will mean fruitful labor for me. Yet what shall I choose? I do not know! I am torn between the two: I

desire to depart and be with Christ, which is better by far; but it is more necessary for you that I remain in the body."
Philippians 1:21-24

Paul knew what joy was waiting for him in Heaven. He chose rightly in saying it would be better for him to be with Christ, but he knew that he still had work to do here on earth. Paul never took his eyes off the real prize. He bore fruit on earth and knew that his real reward was waiting for him in Heaven.

We need to remember that this world is not all that there is. Our eternal reward is in Heaven. Yes, God has work for us to do here and yes, God gives good gifts while we are here on earth. We need to know that nothing will compare to being in His presence for eternity. We were created to glorify Him forever. That is what our entire earthly lives should be moving towards.

HOW WE REMEMBER

If you knew you would die tomorrow, how would you live differently today?

1. We can live our lives with the end in mind. We can know that our death is always before us, not in a morbid way, but in a way that makes us live life on purpose.
2. We can work for treasure that lasts here on earth. We don't need to chase popularity, success, or anything else. We should chase Jesus!
3. We can purposefully have conversations with our loved ones about death that will help prepare for their deaths.

Gospel Rhythm: Repeat Gospel Truths

> *"Satan doesn't control us with fang marks on the flesh but with lies in the heart. Our best defense in the fight against his lies is not the production of incantations but the rehearsal of truth."* - Tim Keller

Introduction

In the evenings, our dog Tink can see his reflection in the patio doors. This inevitably makes him lose his mind barking at himself. We try to comfort him and tell him that it's just his reflection, but he has no way of understanding that. I can also find myself losing my mind over things that aren't true. I start to believe that I need to fit into a non-existent standard. I start misinterpreting God and believe that He doesn't know what is best for me or that He doesn't love me. These beliefs are untrue in the same way that Tink's reflection is not a dog coming to attack him. Just like it is hard for Tink to stop barking at His reflection, it is hard for me to believe truth rather than lies.

We are all saturated in the world's wisdom. From the time we are born, we are inundated with the world's ideas of what makes a person successful, how to live a good life, and the world's ways of right and wrong. We often don't even realize how many wrongful patterns of thinking have made connections through our brains.

Paul tells the Corinthian church:

"Do not deceive yourselves. If any of you think you are wise by the standards of this age, you should become 'fools' so that you may become wise. For the wisdom of this world is foolishness in God's sight. As it is written: 'He catches the wise in their craftiness'; and again, 'The Lord knows that the thoughts of the wise are futile'" (1 Corinthians 3:18-20).

Many of us are content to soak in the world's ideas because we either don't recognize that we are embracing wrongful patterns of thinking, or we don't know how to stop these patterns of thinking. Sometimes we just don't want to swim upstream. We want to be comfortable. Dismantling harmful patterns of thought that have been with us since birth seems like a pretty uncomfortable task. Unless we put in the work to replace these harmful thoughts, we will be plagued with them our entire lives.

Here is an example from my life: when I was in high school, I wasn't getting a lot of playing time on the basketball team. I came home crying one day because I believed that if I wasn't getting playing time, I was less valuable than the other girls on the team. I believed my parents wouldn't be proud of me and I felt unworthy of their love. As I talked things out with them, they replaced the lies I was buying into with the truth. They didn't complain about my coaches, because it was right that I wasn't getting a lot of playing time. I wasn't aggressive or really that athletic, and there were better athletes on the team. My parents told me that they loved me and were proud of me no matter how I performed. They also told me that I had two choices: 1. I could practice more to try to earn a spot with more playing time, or I could 2. Keep doing what I was doing and enjoy playing basketball without getting much playing time in the games. My parents assured me that whichever choice I made, they would be at every game cheering me on and being proud of me.

What wrongful thoughts are you buying into? I would encourage all of us to examine our thoughts and replace the wrongful thoughts with the truth in God's Word. In my own life, one of the results of reading God's Word all the way through was the revelation of wrongful thought patterns and exposure to the truth. I am not the center of the universe, and God loves me not as a result of my actions, but because I am His chosen child.

In the rest of this chapter, we will discuss four common areas where we have wrongful patterns of thinking: our appearances, when we feel rejected, when we are disappointed, and when we worry. We will discuss common misconceptions in each area and then replace those lies with the truth of Scripture. I will provide Bible verses for you to repeat to yourself when you struggle with wrongful patterns of thinking in these areas.

When We Worry About Our Appearance
Our culture is heavily focused on appearances. We are inundated with images of photoshopped people and advertisements

that claim to have the secrets to looking younger. There are filters that can make our appearance look better than it actually is, and all of these messages tell us that we need to look good or we will be considered unworthy.

In my own life, I don't always like what I see when I look in the mirror. It can be easy to pick myself apart and worry about what the world will think of my appearance. I am susceptible to advertisements telling me that I need to be more (fill in the blank). When I start to feel like the world's message is getting louder than God's, I remind myself that God's opinion is the one that matters. I replace the messages of the world with the truth from God's Word.

The verses below are meant to encourage you and help you replace the lies you have been believing with truth from God. The next time you are getting ready and want to pick apart your appearance, think about these verses and how God thinks of you instead of trying to perceive how the world will think of you.

Scripture addresses appearance in several places. The first place we will discuss is in 1 Samuel chapter 16.

1. Samuel is charged by God to go and anoint the next king of Israel from the sons of a man named Jesse. As Samuel starts meeting the sons, he expects the firstborn, Eliab, to be the right choice. God responds by saying, "Do not consider his appearance or his height, for I have rejected him. The Lord does not look at the things man looks at. Man looks at the outward appearance, but the Lord looks at the heart" (1 Samuel 16:7). Seven of Jesse's sons were presented before Samuel be-

fore he knew God's clear choice was David (the youngest and smallest).

In a world where our appearance is all we seem to be judged by, God looks at our hearts. It would do us well to tuck these words away in our hearts and repeat them over and over again.

2. The Bible tells us about Jesus' appearance in Isaiah 53. In Isaiah's prophecy about the coming Messiah, His appearance was described like this: "He had no beauty or majesty to attract us to him, nothing in his appearance that we should desire him" (Isaiah 53:2b). We are told over and over again that we are to imitate our Savior. "Whoever claims to live in him must walk as Jesus did" (1 John 2:6). If Jesus didn't have anything about His appearance to attract us to Him, should we be super concerned about our appearance attracting others to ourselves?

3. The disciple Peter wrote a letter to encourage early Christians about holy living in times of persecution. One of his instructions was about not being hyper-focused on appearance: "Your beauty should not come from adornment, such as braided hair and the wearing of gold jewelry and fine clothes. Instead, it should be that of your inner self, the unfading beauty of a gentle and quiet spirit, which is of great worth in God's sight. For this is the way holy women of the past who put their hope in God used to make themselves beautiful" (1 Peter 3:3-5).

The Bible does refer to women as beautiful, but beauty is never the main focus. Esther was beautiful to get the king's ear to save her people. Rahab was beautiful, and she was in the hall of faith in Hebrews 11 with no mention of her beauty. Make no mistake. God does everything for His glory. Our outward beauty or lack thereof is all part of God's plan. We are to glorify God with the bodies that we have been given.

When We Feel Rejected

Many of us have felt the stab of rejection. When Jesus walked the earth as a man, He felt the stab of rejection as well (Matthew 10:24-26). Human beings are fragile creatures. We are all asking the question, "Am I worthy?" When we ask this question to the people in our lives rather than God, we give people more authority over us than they should have. God is our authority. God is the only one that can answer the question, "Am I worthy?"

We know the answer to the question already. We have all sinned and fallen short of the glory of God, which makes us unworthy. Because God loves us, He sent His Son to dress us in a righteousness that is not our own. Jesus's life, death, and resurrection made a way for those with repentant faith in Him to be deemed worthy. We are worthy because of Jesus.

1. Jesus warned the disciples that He was going to die: "And he said, 'The Son of Man must suffer many things and be rejected by the elders, the chief priests and the teachers of the law, and he must be killed and on the third day be raised to life'" (Luke 9:22). Jesus experienced rejection while He was on earth. We also will experience rejection if we are to follow Him. "If you belonged to the world, it would love you as its own. As

it is, you do not belong to the world, but I have chosen you out of the world. That is why the world hates you" (John 15:19). The next time you feel rejected, remember that Jesus has felt our pain and understands what it is to be rejected. We also need to remember that when we are in Jesus, we always have a place with Him. If the world rejects us, we remember that our place is with Jesus. We don't have to get bogged down in that rejection. We remember we have an eternal hope waiting for us.

2. We belong to and are loved by Jesus. When we belong to Jesus, we are free to obey Him and submit to His authority on earth. "So, my brothers and sisters, you also died to the law through the body of Christ, that you might belong to another, to him who was raised from the dead, in order that we might bear fruit for God" (Romans 7:4). "If we live, we live for the Lord; and if we die, we die for the Lord. So, whether we live or die, we belong to the Lord" (Romans 14:8). People may reject us, but we have a place with Jesus. We are also loved by Him. "For God so loved the world that he gave his one and only Son, that whoever believes in him shall not perish but have eternal life" (John 3:16).

3. Christians all over the world are in one family. We belong to each other and we are no longer rejected because we have a family. "So in Christ we, though many, form one body, and each member belongs to all the others" (Romans 12:5). We are in a body that is able to build us up and spur us along on our faith journeys. It is our job to care for each other on this side of Heaven. "Con-

sequently, you are no longer foreigners and strangers, but fellow citizens with God's people and also members of his household, built on the foundation of the apostles and prophets, with Christ Jesus himself as the chief cornerstone. In him, the whole building is joined together and rises to become a holy temple in the Lord. And in him you too are being built together to become a dwelling in which God lives by his Spirit" (Ephesians 2:19-22). Jesus tells us when we lose homes and family that we will be provided those things by the body of Christ (His church) all over the world (Mark 10:29-30).

When We Feel Disappointed

The NCAA basketball tournament displays the idea of disappointment in a very palpable way. There are two themes running through the tournament: hope and disappointment. Every team in the tournament has the hope that they will have their one shining moment. Only one team will experience the hope of winning the tournament coming to fruition. The other teams will be left disappointed. I see these two themes spilling out into our daily lives as well. We all have hope that things will go well with us. We hope that everything will turn out the way we want it to. Disappointment is also a big theme in our lives. Living on this earth for even a short amount of time teaches us that not everything goes the way that we want it to. We are going to come up short in the way that we expect things to go.

Life on this earth will be filled with disappointment. We are not going to get everything we want. Disappointment is most prominent when we put our hope in the wrong things. We get into trouble because we place our hope in wins, vacations, people, etc... We aren't putting our hope in the Only Hope.

Here is what God's Word says about disappointment:

- "Therefore, since we have a great high priest who has ascended into heaven, Jesus the Son of God, let us hold firmly to the faith we profess. For we do not have a high priest who is unable to empathize with our weaknesses, but we have one who has been tempted in every way, just as we are—yet he did not sin. Let us then approach God's throne of grace with confidence, so that we may receive mercy and find grace to help us in our time of need" (Hebrews 4:14-16). Jesus came as a man and experienced everything we experience here on earth. He was rejected and disappointed. We don't have a high priest who is unable to sympathize with our weakness. Jesus understands how we are feeling.
- We can talk to our own souls and remind ourselves that our hope is in God. "Why, my soul, are you downcast? Why so disturbed within me? Put your hope in God, for I will yet praise him, my Savior and my God" (Psalm 42:11). When nothing in this world makes sense, we can point our souls to God and put our trust in Him.
- We no doubt will be disappointed in this earth. We will feel the sting of life in a fallen world. When we are in Christ, we will have life! "The thief comes only to steal and kill and destroy; I have come that they may have life, and have it to the full" (John 10:10).

When We Worry

Worry is like a rocking chair: you keep moving, but it doesn't get you anywhere. When we worry, we are anxiously toiling and not resting, but we aren't solving any of our problems. It was a hard realization for me that worry in my life is sin. I told myself that I couldn't stop myself from worrying, that it was a natural reaction to the world around me. The reason sin is a worry is because we are not placing our trust in God. We are trying to figure things out for ourselves and be self-sufficient. We are supposed to live lives in dependence on God and rest in Him. He will provide all that we need. "I sought the Lord, and he answered me; he delivered me from all my fears" (Psalm 34:4).

God is the only one with the power to deliver us from our fears. We don't have that kind of power, and yet we wear ourselves out trying to deliver ourselves. God sovereignly knows what is best for us. He will deliver us, we can't.

"Therefore I tell you, do not worry about your life, what you will eat or drink; or about your body, what you will wear. Is not life more than food, and the body more than clothes? Look at the birds of the air; they do not sow or reap or store away in barns, and yet your heavenly Father feeds them. Are you not much more valuable than they? Can any one of you by worrying add a single hour to your life? And why do you worry about clothes? See how the flowers of the field grow. They do not labor or spin. Yet I tell you that not even Solomon in all his splendor was dressed like one of these. If that is how God clothes the grass of the field, which is here today and tomorrow is thrown into the fire, will he not much more clothe you—you of little faith? So do not worry, saying, 'What shall we eat?' or

'What shall we drink?' or 'What shall we wear?' For the pagans run after all these things, and your heavenly Father knows that you need them. But seek first his Kingdom and his righteousness, and all these things will be given to you as well. Therefore do not worry about tomorrow, for tomorrow will worry about itself. Each day has enough trouble of its own" (Matthew 6:25-34). I feel such conviction when I read this passage. It points out how often I worry about the trivial things in this life. I worry about what I will eat, what I will wear, and how things will work out. God has shown me time and again that He will be the one who provides and that I don't need to worry. It is good for us to be reminded in Scripture over and over again that we don't need to worry. If worry is a struggle in your life, take these Scriptures with you. Remember that God is the one who feeds the birds and takes care of us.

"Do not be anxious about anything, but in every situation, by prayer and petition, with thanksgiving, present your requests to God" (Philippians 4:6). God doesn't just leave us with the command to not be anxious, but He lovingly allows us to present our requests to Him. We can stop worrying because we can give Him our burdens and He will shoulder the load.

God's Word and the Holy Spirit living in us help us to separate truth from lies. When we arm ourselves with Scripture, we can remember what is true. I would like to challenge you to study the Scriptures and apply them to your life. Write verses down or memorize the verses that will help with whatever situation you are facing. When we have God's Word guiding us, we can face any obstacle knowing that God is with us, He loves us, and He empowers us to do whatever we need to do.

An Affirmation

Affirmations have become quite popular in recent years. I see parents placing videos on social media and having their children repeat affirmations: I am strong, I am capable, I am loved. I am not condemning affirmations because I think that speaking good thoughts to our minds is a good thing. My concern with these types of affirmations is that we are relying on our own strength rather than God's strength. Our strength will fail, but God's strength will not.

I would like to provide an affirmation for you to repeat that is filled with truth and can help us to reorient when our minds start to fill with lies.

Who Am I?

I am God's child: "See what great love the Father has lavished on us, that we should be called children of God! And that is what we are! The reason the world does not know us is that it did not know him. Dear friends, now we are children of God, and what we will be has not yet been made known. But we know that when Christ appears, we shall be like him, for we shall see him as he is" (1 John 3:1-2).

Being children of God allows us to rest in Him, knowing that we aren't strong and capable on our own, but we are dearly loved.

One of our kids has been having some trouble falling asleep at night. It seems like this child can't keep the scary thoughts away. We are trying to train our child's brain to think about good things. As with many of the lessons I teach my children, I need to learn to think about good things as well. Repeating gospel truths to ourselves in an excellent way to keep our minds thinking rightful thoughts about our lives.

> **HOW WE REMEMBER**
>
> Do you struggle with your appearance, rejection, disappointment, and worry? Where do you run in those times?
>
> We are immersed in a hostile environment. The world does not love the things of God. We will be bombarded with the world's messages, and we need to arm ourselves with the truth of God's Word.
>
> Here are some action steps you can take when you feel weary.
>
> 1. Examine your heart. What is causing you to feel weary? Is it one of the four categories we discussed in this chapter? Is it something else? Ask God to reveal to you why you are feeling weary.
> 2. After you identify why you are weary, turn to Scripture. What does God's Word tell you about what you are feeling?
> 3. Write those verses down and commit them to memory. Whenever that wearying thing comes up you can fight those feelings by rehearsing the Truth. The Psalmist writes: "Why, my soul, are you downcast? Why so disturbed within me? Put your hope in God, for I will yet praise him, my Savior and my God" (Psalm 42:11). We ask our souls why they are downcast and then we put our hope in God by filling up on His Truth.
> 4. Finally, we entrust ourselves to God. We surrender to His loving care in our lives and we know that we are being held by Him. Jesus gives a wonderful example of this: "When they hurled their insults at him, he did not retaliate; when he suffered, he made no threats. Instead, he entrusted himself to him who judges justly" (1 Peter 2:23).

Epilogue

I hope that reading this book has helped you breathe a sigh of relief, knowing that you aren't alone in your Christian walk. I am right there with you in my Christian forgetfulness. When I forget, I tend to beat myself up. I say things to myself like: "You should be farther along in your journey than you are" and "You should be more mature in your faith than you are." When guilt starts to overtake me, God has mercifully shown me that I can come back to Him and ask for His help with whatever I am facing. I don't need to beat myself up for being forgetful, I can praise God that He shows me mercy in my forgetfulness.

One of the best parts about having faith in Jesus is that He will continue to work on us our entire lives. My favorite reminder of this is in Philippians 1:6: "Being confident of this, that he who began a good work in you will carry it on to completion until the day of Christ Jesus."

Part of how God keeps working on us is by giving us these gospel rhythms to practice so that we can draw near to Him. In the same way that household chores cleaning, laundry, cooking, and dishes need to be repeated over and over again, we need to repeat the gospel rhythms to help us draw nearer to God our entire lives.

> "Submit yourselves, then, to God. Resist the devil, and he will flee from you. Come near to God and he will come near to you."
> James 4:7-8a

I hope that you will cling to God's truths in a world that doesn't. Satan is going to try to take us off of our journey in the same way that Apollyon tried to take Christian off the path in *Pilgrim's Progress*. We can walk through this life knowing that God is the one leading us and protecting us.

> "Therefore, since we are surrounded by such a great cloud of witnesses, let us throw off everything that hinders and the sin that so easily entangles. And let us run with perseverance the race marked out for us, fixing our eyes on Jesus, the pioneer and perfecter of faith. For the joy set before him he endured the cross, scorning its shame, and sat down at the right hand of the throne of God. Consider him who endured such opposition from sinners, so that you will not grow weary and lose heart."
> Hebrews 12:1-3

Acknowledgments

Thank you to Abby McDonald for being a wonderful cheerleader and editing this book.

Mom and Dad, I am so thankful for how you have helped me understand God's unfailing love for me in your love for me. Though your love isn't perfect like God's is, it has pointed me to His love over and over again. Thank you for your love and support.

Grandma Wellman, I feel the same about your unconditional love and support for me as well. You and Grandpa pointed me to God's love as well and I am so thankful for your influence on my life.

Emily, Caleb, Nora, and Elizabeth, you are the best kids a mom could ask for. I am so thankful for the way that you allowed me time to write and have been so helpful in this whole process. I am so proud of the young ladies and man you are becoming.

Peter, when I think about it I can't fully understand why I get to be married to the man of my dreams and my best friend. I love being your teammate and walking through life together. I am so thankful for your support not only in this project but in all of life.

References

[1] As I write this nonfiction book, I feel it models the *Pilgrim's Progress* fiction book. Christian is walking the path to the Celestial City but ends up having to get back on the right path over and over again, just like us. Bunyan, John. Pilgrim's Progress. Oxford University Press, 2008.

[2] "What is our only hope in life and death?" New City Catechism, Crossway, accessed 7 Apr. 2024, http://newcitycatechism.com/new-city-catechism/#4.

[3] "The Westminster Larger Catechism." *Ligonier Ministries*, accessed 7 Apr. 2024, https://www.ligonier.org/learn/articles/westminster-larger-catechism.

[4] "Heidelberg Catechism." *Westminster Theological Seminary*, accessed 7 Apr. 2024, https://students.wts.edu/resources/creeds/heidelberg.html.

[5] Studd, C.T. "Only One Life." 1904.

[6] "Heidelberg Catechism." *Westminster Theological Seminary*, accessed 7 Apr. 2024, https://students.wts.edu/resources/creeds/heidelberg.html.

[7] Wilkin, Jen, Better (Lifeway Press, 2019), 11.

[8] "Short Animated Bible Videos," Bible Project, accessed April 7, 2024, https://bibleproject.com/explore/

[9] Townend, Stuart. "How Deep the Father's Love for Us." 1995.

[10] Aquinas, Thomas. *Summa Theologica*. Espasa Calpe, 1996.

[11] Bunyan, John. *Grace Abounding to the Chief of Sinners*. Digireads.com, 2011.

[12] *Merriam-Webster's Collegiate Dictionary*. Merriam-Webster, 11th ed., 2003.

[13] Pink, A.W. *Repentance: What Saith the Scriptures?* Chapel Library, [no known date].

[14] Bainton, Roland H. *Here I Stand: A Life of Martin Luther*. Abingdon-Cokesbury Press, 1950.

[15] "Life, Art, and Creativity with Andrew Peterson." *Journeywomen*, accessed 9 Apr. 2024, https://www.journeywomen.org/episode/life-art-creativity.

[16] "Pray." *Radical*, accessed 12 Jan. 2014, https://radical.net/message/pray/.

[17] Pierson, Arthur Tappan. *George Muller of Bristol*. Hendrickson Publishers, 2014.

[18] "Shop." *ValMarie Paper*, accessed 9 Apr. 2024, https://shop.valmariepaper.com/collections/journal-collection.

[19] "Charles Spurgeon is often attributed with saying, 'I have learned to kiss the wave that throws me against the Rock of Ages,' though the exact source remains unconfirmed."

[20] "Grief Should Always Make Us Better." *Challies*, accessed 5 Jan. 2021, https://www.challies.com/articles/grief-should-always-make-us-better/.

[21] Wurmbrand, Richard. *Tortured for Christ*. Magdalene Press, 2015.

[22] "Heidelberg Catechism." *Westminster Theological Seminary*, accessed 7 Apr. 2024, https://students.wts.edu/resources/creeds/heidelberg.html.

[23] Augustine. *Augustine's Confessions*. Translated by R.S. Pine-Coffin, Penguin Classics, 1961.

[24] Buttrick, George Arthur, editor. *The Interpreter's Dictionary of the Bible*. Abingdon Press, 1962, p. 678.

[25] Berry, Wendell. *This Day: Collected and New Sabbath Poems*. Counterpoint, 2014.

REFERENCES

[26] Bonar, Andrew. *Robert Murray M'Cheyne: Memoir and Remains.* Banner of Truth and Trust, 1966.

[27] Credited to Heraclitus

[28] Merriam-Webster's Collegiate Dictionary. Merriam-Webster, 11th ed., 2003.

[29] Crosby, Fanny. "Near the Cross." 1869.

[30] *Chariots of Fire.* Directed by Hugh Hudson, TCF/Allied Stars/Enigma, 1981.

[31] Keith and Kristyn Getty sing a *Hymn of the Month* with their family and we were pleased to incorporate their idea into our family worship time.

[32] Willard, Kelly. "I Will Cast All My Cares Upon You." 1981.

[33] Lewis, C.S. *The Lion, the Witch and the Wardrobe.* S French, 1987.

[34] Trantham, Cara Cobble. *Hymns: A Study on Classic Hymns.* Daily Grace Co, 2017.

[35] "Jaime." Disney Parks Advertisement. YouTube, Accessed 9 Apr. 2024, https://www.youtube.com/watch?v=4xrhIWGCee0.

[36] Athanasius. *On the Incarnation.* Dead Authors Society, 2018.

[37] Keller, Timothy. Facebook, 2023, Accessed 19 May 2023.

[38] Joey + Rory. *Hymns.* Gaither Music, 2016.

Printed in the USA
CPSIA information can be obtained
at www.ICGtesting.com
CBHW020516150924
14364CB00002B/15

9 798891 851023